Facts about Korea

Copyright © 2003, 1973
by Korean Overseas Information Service

All rights reserved.

Originally published in 1973
by Korean Overseas Information Service

Revised edition, 2003
Third printing, 2005
by Hollym Corporation; Publishers
Phone: (908) 353-1655   Fax: (908) 353-0255
http://www.hollym.com

Published simultaneously in Korea
13-13 Gwancheol-dong, Jongno-gu, Seoul 110-111, Korea
Phone: (02) 735-7551~4   Fax: (02) 730-5149, 8192
http://www.hollym.co.kr   e-mail: info@hollym.co.kr

ISBN: 1-56591-209-8

Printed in Korea

Facts *about* Korea

HOLLYM

Elizabeth, NJ · Seoul

Foreword

The phrase "Dynamic Korea" is Korea's new national motto that embodies the modern, energetic image of a nation that rose from the ashes of war to become an economic powerhouse in Asia. It also represents the pride of the Korean people who have achieved liberal democracy and economic prosperity.

Korea's growth-oriented, export-led economic development since the 1960s was so remarkable that it earned the expression, "the Miracle on the Hangang River," in the 1970s. Subsequently, Seoul has successfully hosted the 24th Olympics in 1988 and Korea co-hosted the 2002 FIFA World Cup soccer finals with Japan. Through these occasions, we have demonstrated to the world our rich cultural heritage and love of art, as well as modern technologies. The size of the Korean economy today ranks 12th in the world, and Korea is working hard to become a world economic leader in the new millennium.

Also, Korea is constantly improving the overall business environment as Northeast Asia's new business center and logistics hub. Taking advantage of our geographical location between such large economies as China and Japan, we expect to emerge as a major economic and IT power early in this century.

The Republic of Korea has steadily followed the path to mature democracy and market economy. Even though the legacies of the Cold War still linger on this peninsula, Korea today is poised to make a new economic take-off. We are also building a durable structure of peace on the Korean Peninsula and promoting common prosperity for South and North Korea through peace, reconciliation and cooperation.

We hope that this handbook is helpful to those who wish to understand Korea, its land and people. We also hope that you will come and visit this "Dynamic Korea, the Hub of Asia."

CONTENTS

Geography and People
Geography   9
Climate   11
People and Population   13
Language   14

History
Unified Silla and Balhae   18
Goryeo   19
Joseon   21
Japanese Occupation and Korea's Independence Movement   24
The Founding of the Republic of Korea   26

Constitution and Government
The Constitution   29
The President   32
The Executive Branch   34
Legislature   37
Judiciary   40
The Constitutional Court   42
Local Government   43

Inter-Korean Relations
Historical Background   46
Inter-Korean Exchanges and Cooperation   48
The Roh Moo-hyun Administration's Policy of Inter-Korean
Reconciliation and Cooperation   49

Korea in the World
Korea's International Relations   53
Korea's International Economic Relations   54
Diplomatic Activities for International Peace and Cooperation   56
The Roh Moo-hyun Administration's Policy for Peace and
Prosperity in Northeast Asia   60

Economy
Economic Growth   62
Industrial Development   65
Science and Technology   70
Economic Challenges   72
Financial Restructuring   73
Corporate Restructuring   75
Other Measures   76
Environment for Foreign Investment   77
Capital Market Liberalization   80
Investor-Oriented Support System   81
Outlook for the Economy   84

Social Welfare
Employment   85
Housing   88
Health and Medical Services   89
Social Security   91
Women   93

Education
Overview   96
The School System   96
Special Education and Non-formal Education   101
Korean Studies   102

Transportation and Communications
Transportation   104
Communications   110

The Media
Newspapers and News Agencies   115
Television   116
Radio   118

Culture and the Arts
UNESCO's World Heritage List   121
Fine Arts   125
Literature   131
Painting   133
Music and Dance   137
Drama and Movies   141
Museums and Theaters   146

Korean Lifestyle
Family Life   155
Names   156
Festivals   157
National Holidays   160

Religion
Shamanism   162
Buddhism   163
Confucianism   165
Catholicism   167
Protestantism   168
Cheondogyo   170
Islam   170

Sports and Leisure
The Seoul Olympics in Retrospect   173
International Sports Competition   174
2002 FIFA World Cup Korea/Japan   175
National Sports Events   178
Others   179
Traditional Sports   180
Leisure   183

Tourism
Getting to Korea   188
Exploring Korea   190
Travel Advice   207
Accommodations   209
How to Travel Around Korea   210
Shopping   212

20 Korean Cultural Features   216

Geography and People

Geography

Korea is situated on the Korean Peninsula, which spans 1,100 kilometers north to south. The Korean Peninsula lies on the northeastern section of the Asian continent, where Korean waters are joined by the western-most parts of the Pacific. The peninsula shares its northern border with China and Russia. To its east is the East Sea, beyond which neighboring Japan lies. In addition to the mainland peninsula, Korea includes some 3,000 islands.

Korea encompasses a total of 222,154 square kilometers-almost the same size as Britain or Rumania. Some 45 percent of this area, or 99,000 square kilometers, is considered cultivatable area, excluding reclaimed land areas. Mountainous terrain accounts for some two-thirds of the territory like Portugal, Hungary or Ireland.

The Mt. Taebaeksan range runs the full length of the east coast, where the lashing waves of the East Sea have carved out sheer cliffs and rocky islets. The western and southern slopes are rather gentle, forming plains and many offshore islands honeycombed with inlets.

The peninsula features so many scenic mountains and rivers that Koreans have often likened their country to a beautifully embroidered brocade. The

Russia

China

Dumangang river

Mt. Baekdusan

Amnokgang river

Mt. Myohyangsan

Cheongcheongang river

Hamheung field

East Sea

Daedonggang river

Pyongyang field

Mt. Geumgangsan

KOREA

Mt. Bukhansan

Mt. Seoraksan

Gimpo field

Seoul

Mt. Odaesan

Ulleungdo

Hangang river

Dokdo

Yellow Sea

Mt. Chiaksan

Mt. Taebaeksan

Mt. Sobaeksan

Mt. Songnisan

Geumgang river

Nakdonggang river

Gimhae field

Mt. Naejangsan

Mt. Jirisan

Naju field

Seomjingang river

Yeongsangang river

Korea Strait

Mt. Hallasan

Jejudo

highest peak is Mt. Baekdusan in North Korea, which rises up 2,744 meters above sea level along the northern border facing China. Mt. Baekdusan is an extinct volcano where a large volcanic lake, named Cheonji, has been formed. The mountain is regarded as an especially important symbol of the Korean spirit and is mentioned in Korea's national anthem.

Considering its territorial size, Korea has a relatively large number of rivers and streams. These waterways played crucial roles in shaping the lifestyle of Koreans, and in the nation's industrialization. The two longest rivers in North Korea are the Amnokgang River (Yalu, 790 kilometers) and the Dumangang River (Tumen, 521 kilometers). These rivers originate from Mt. Baekdusan and flow to the west and the east, respectively. They form the peninsula's northern border.

In the southern part of the peninsula, the Nakdonggang River (525 kilometers) and the Hangang River (514 kilometers) are the two major waterways. The Hangang river flows through Seoul, the capital of Korea, and serves as a lifeline for the heavily concentrated population in the central region of modern Korea, just as it did for the people of the ancient kingdoms that developed along its banks.

Surrounding the peninsula on three sides, the ocean has played an integral role in the life of the Koreans since ancient times, contributing to the early development of shipbuilding and navigational skills.

Climate

Korea has four distinct seasons. Spring and autumn are rather short, summer is hot and humid, and winter is cold and dry with abundant snowfall.

Temperatures differ widely from region to region within Korea, with the average being between 6°C (43°F) and 16°C (61°F). The average temperature in August, the hottest period of the year, ranges from 19°C (66°F) to 27°C (81°F), while in January, the coldest month, temperatures range from -8°C (17°F) to 7°C (43°F).

In early spring the Korean Peninsula experiences "yellow sand / dust" carried by wind from the deserts in northern China. But in mid-April, the country enjoys balmy weather with the mountains and fields garbed in brilliant wild flowers. Farmers prepare seedbeds for the annual rice crop at this time.

Autumn, with its crisp air and crystal blue sky, is the season most widely loved by Koreans. The countryside is particularly beautiful, colored in a diversity of rustic hues. Autumn, the harvest season, features various folk festivals rooted in ancient agrarian customs.

People and Population

Koreans are one ethnic family and speak one language. Sharing distinct physical characteristics, they are believed to be descendants of several Mongol tribes that migrated onto the Korean Peninsula from Central Asia.

In the seventh century, the various states of the peninsula were unified for the first time under the Silla Kingdom (57 B.C.-A.D. 935). Such homogeneity has enabled Koreans to be relatively free from ethnic problems and to maintain a firm solidarity with one another.

As of the end of 2002, Korea's total population was estimated at 47,640,000 with a density of 479 people per square kilometer. The population of North Korea is estimated to be 22,253,000.

Korea saw its population grow by an annual rate of 3 percent during the 1960s, but growth slowed to 2 percent over the next decade. Today, the rate stands at 0.6 percent, and is expected to further decline to 0.06 percent by 2020.

A notable trend in Korea's demographics is that it

is growing older with each passing year. Statistics show that 6.9 percent of the total population of Korea was 65 years or older in 1999 and 7.9 percent of the total in 2002.

In the 1960s, Korea's population distribution formed a pyramid shape, with a high birth rate and relatively short life expectancy. However, the structure is now shaped more like a bell with a low birth rate and extended life expectancy. Youth (under the age of 15 years) will make up a decreasing portion of the total, while senior citizens (65 years or older) will account for some 15.1 percent of the total by the year 2020.

The nation's rapid industrialization and urbanization in the 1960s and 1970s has been accompanied by continuing migration of rural residents into the cities, particularly Seoul, resulting in heavily populated metropolitan areas. However, in recent years, an increasing number of people have begun moving to suburban areas of Seoul.

Language

All Koreans speak and write the same language, which has been a decisive factor in forging their strong national identity. Koreans have developed several different dialects in addition to the standard used in Seoul. However, the dialects, except for that of Jeju-do province, are similar enough for native speakers to understand without any difficulties.

Linguistic and ethnological studies have classified the Korean language in the Altaic language family, which includes the Turkic, Mongolic and Tungus-Manchu languages.

The Korean Alphabet *Hangeul*, was created by King Sejong the Great during the 15th century.

The Korean Alphabet

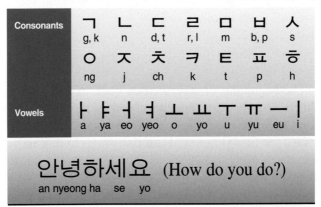

Consonants	ㄱ	ㄴ	ㄷ	ㄹ	ㅁ	ㅂ	ㅅ
	g, k	n	d, t	r, l	m	b, p	s
	ㅇ	ㅈ	ㅊ	ㅋ	ㅌ	ㅍ	ㅎ
	ng	j	ch	k	t	p	h
Vowels	ㅏ	ㅑ	ㅓ	ㅕ	ㅗ	ㅛ	ㅜ	ㅠ	ㅡ	ㅣ
	a	ya	eo	yeo	o	yo	u	yu	eu	i

안녕하세요 (How do you do?)
an nyeong ha se yo

Before its creation, only a relatively small percentage of the population could master the Chinese characters due to their difficulty.

In attempting to invent a Korean writing system, King Sejong looked to several writing systems known at the time, such as old Chinese seal characters and Uighur and Mongolian scripts.

The system that they came up with, however, is predominantly based upon phonological studies. Above all, they developed and followed a theory of tripartite division of the syllable into initial, medial and final phonemes, as opposed to the bipartite division of traditional Chinese phonology.

Hangeul which consists of 10 vowels and 14 consonants, can be combined to form numerous syllabic groupings. It is simple, yet systematic and comprehensive, and is considered one of the most scientific writing systems in the world. *Hangeul* is easy to learn and write, which has greatly contributed to Korea's high literacy rate and advanced publication industry.

History

The beginning of Korea dates back to 2333 B.C., when *Dangun*, the legendary son of the Heavenly God and a woman from a bear-totem tribe, established the first kingdom. Historians refer to this earliest era of Korean history as the Gojoseon (Ancient Joseon) period.

Ancient Korea was characterized by clan communities that combined to form small town-states.

The town-states gradually united into tribal leagues with complex political structures, which eventually grew into kingdoms. Among various tribal leagues, Goguryeo (37 B.C.- A.D. 668), situated along the middle course of the Amnokgang River (Yalu), was the first to mature into a kingdom.

Goguryeo Kingdom (5th Century)

Goguryeo's aggressive troops conquered neighboring tribes one after another, and in 313, they even occupied China's Lolang outposts. Baekje (18 B.C.-A.D. 660), which grew out of a town-state located south of the Hangang

Chronological Table

	KOREA	CHINA	THE WEST
B.C			
	Paleolithic Age		
	Neolithic Age		
5,000	Bronze Age	Bronze Age	Early Mesopotamia
	Gojoseon		Egyptian Kingdoms
2,000			
		Shang Dynasty (1766~1122)	
1,000		Zhou (1122~256)	
		Spring and Autumn Era (770~476)	Greek Civilization
		Iron Age	Founding of Rome (735)
500	Iron Age	Warring States Era (475~221)	Socrates (469~399)
	Buyeo	Qin Dynasty (221~206)	Alexander the Great (356~323)
		Western Han Dynasty	First Punic War (264~241)
		(206 B.C.~A.D. 25)	Second Punic War (219~201)
200	Confederated Kingdoms of		Jullius Ceasar (101~44)
	Samhan (three Han States)		
100			
	Three Kingdoms:		
	Silla (57 B.C.~A.D. 935)		Birth of Jesus Christ
	Goguryeo (37 B.C.~A.D. 668)		
	Baekje (18 B.C.~A.D. 660)		
A.D			
200	Gaya (42~562)	Eastern Han Dynasty (25~220)	
		San Guo (Three Kingdoms)	
		Era (220~280)	
		Jin Dynasty (265~420)	
300			Christianity established as state
			religion of Roman Empire (392)
			Roman Empire split in two (395)
400		Nan Bei Chao Dynasties	Anglo-Saxon established
		(420~589)	in Britain (449)
500		Sui Dynasty (581~618)	Mohammed (570~632)
600			
	Unified Silla Kingdom (668~935)	Tang Dynasty (618~907)	Hegira (662) and beginning
	Balhae Kingdom (698~926)		of Islamic era
700			
			Charles the Great crowned
			first Holy Roman Emperor
900	Goryeo Dynasty (918~1392)	Wu Dai Dynasties (907~960)	
		Song Dynasty (960~1279)	
1000			
			First Crusade (1096~99)
1100		Yuan Dynasty (1206~1368)	Magna Carta (1215)
			Marco Polo (1254~1324)
1300	Joseon Dynasty (1392~1910)	Ming Dynasty (1368~1644)	The Hundred Years' War
			(1334~1434)
1400			Gutenberg's Press (1434)
			Columbus discovered
			America (1492)
1500			Martin Luther launched reform
			of the Church (1517)
1600		Qing Dynasty (1616~1911)	The Thirty Years' War (1618~48)
1700			American Independence (1776)
			French Revolution (1789~1793)
1800	Daehan Empire		American Civil War (1861~65)
1900	Annexation by Japan (1910)	Establishment of the	World War I (1914~18)
	Establishment of the	Republic of China (1912)	World War II (1939~45)
	Republic of Korea (1948)	Establishment of the People's	
		Republic of China (1949)	

River in the vicinity of present-day Seoul, was another confederated kingdom similar to Goguryeo. During the reign of King Geunchogo (r. 346-375), Baekje developed into a centralized and aristocratic state.

The Silla Kingdom (57 B.C.-A.D. 935) was located the furthest south on the peninsula, and was initially the weakest and most underdeveloped of the Three Kingdoms. However, because it was geographically removed from Chinese influence, it was more open to non-Chinese practices and ideas. Its society was markedly class-oriented and later developed the unique Hwarang (Flower of Youth) Corps as well as an advanced Buddhist practice.

Unified Silla and Balhae

By the mid-sixth century, the Silla Kingdom had brought under its control all of the neighboring Gaya Kingdoms, a group of fortified town-states that had developed in the southeastern region of the peninsula from the mid-first century to the mid-sixth century. Silla also effected a military alliance with Tang China to subjugate the Goguryeo and Baekje Kingdoms. Subsequently, Silla fought against Tang China when the latter exposed its ambition to incorporate the territories of Goguryeo and Baekje.

Silla repelled the Chinese in 676. Then in 698, the former people of Goguryeo who resided in south-central Manchuria established the Kingdom of Balhae. Balhae included not only people of Goguryeo, but also a large Malgal population.

Balhae established a government system centered around five regional capitals, which was modeled after the Goguryeo Kingdom's administrative structure. Balhae possessed an advanced culture which was rooted in that of Goguryeo.

Balhae prosperity reached its height in the first half of the ninth century with the occupation of a vast territory reaching to the Amur river in the north and Kaiyuan in south-central Manchuria to the west. It also established diplomatic ties with Turkey and Japan. Balhae existed until 926, when it was overthrown by the Khitan. Then many of the ruling class, who were mostly Koreans, moved south and joined the newly founded Goryeo Dynasty.

Balhae and Unified Silla (8th century)

Silla unified the Korean Peninsula in 668 and saw the zenith of their power and prosperity in the mid-eighth century. It attempted to establish an ideal Buddhist country. The Bulguksa temple was constructed during the Unified Silla period. However, the state cult of Buddhism began to deteriorate as the nobility indulged in luxury. Also there was conflict among regional leaders who claimed authority over the occupied kingdoms of Goguryeo and Baekje. In 935, the king of Silla formally surrendered to the court of the newly founded Goryeo Dynasty.

Goryeo

Despite frequent foreign invasions, the Korean

The Goryeo Dynasty (11th century)

Peninsula has been ruled by a single government since the Silla unification in 668 while maintaining its political independence and cultural and ethnic heritage. Both the Goryeo (r. 918-1392) and the Joseon (r. 1392-1910) Dynasties consolidated their authority and flourished culturally, while repelling such intruders as the Khitans, Mongols and Japanese. The Goryeo Dynasty was founded by Wang Geon, a general who had served under Gungye, a rebel prince of the Silla Kingdom. Choosing his native town of Songak (the present-day Gaeseong in North Korea) as the capital, Wang Geon proclaimed the goal of recovering the lost territory of the Goguryeo Kingdom in northeast China.

He named his dynasty Goryeo, from which the modern name Korea is derived. Although the Goryeo Dynasty could not reclaim lost lands, it achieved a sophisticated culture represented by *cheongja* or blue-green celadon and flourishing Buddhist tradition. No less significant was the invention of the world's first movable metal type in 1234, which preceded Gutenberg of Germany by two centuries. About that time, Korean skilled artisans also completed the herculean task of carving the entire Buddhist canon on large woodblocks.

Tripitaka Koreana woodblocks in Haeinsa Temple

These woodblocks, numbering more than 80,000, were intended to invoke the influence of Buddha for the repulsion of the Mongol invaders. Called the *Tripitaka Koreana,* they are now stored at the historic Haeinsa temple.

In its later years, the Goryeo Dynasty was weakened by internal struggles among scholar officials and warriors, and between Confucianists and Buddhists. The Mongol incursions that began in

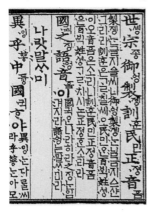

Hunminjeongeum

1231, left Goryeo as a Mongol vassal state for nearly a century despite the courageous resistance from Goryeo's people.

Joseon

In 1392, General Yi Seong-gye established a new dynasty called Joseon. The early rulers of Joseon, in order to counter the dominant Buddhist influence during the Goryeo period, supported Confucianism as the guiding philosophy of the kingdom.

The Joseon rulers governed the dynasty with a well-balanced political system. A civil service examination system was the main channel for recruiting government officials. The examinations served as the backbone for social mobility and intellectual activity during the period. The Confucian-oriented society, however, highly valued academic learning while disdaining commerce and manufacturing.

During the reign of King Sejong the Great (r. 1418-1450), Joseon's fourth monarch, Korea enjoyed an unprecedented flowering of culture and art. Under King Sejong's patronage, scholars at the royal academy created the Korean alphabet, called Hangeul. It was then called *Hunminjeong-eum*, or "proper phonetic system to educate the people."

King Sejong's interest in astronomical science was comprehensive. Sundials, water clocks, celestial globes and astronomical maps were produced at his request. He abdicated the throne to his son, King

The Joseon Dynasty (15th century)

A drawing of *Geobukseon*, believed to be the world's first iron-clad battleship.

Munjong (r. 1450-1452), but his death in 1452 brought an 11-year-old crown prince, Danjong, to the throne.

In 1455, Prince Suyangdaegun, uncle of King Danjong, usurped the throne from the young ruler. Suyangdaegun became King Sejo (r. 1455-1468). He established the institutional framework for government by publishing a compendium of legal codes, called *"Gyeongguk Daejeon."*

In 1592, Japan invaded the Joseon Dynasty to pave the way for its incursion into China. At sea, Admiral Yi Sun-sin (1545-1598), one of the most respected figures in Korean history, led a series of brilliant naval maneuvers against the Japanese, deploying the *Geobukseon* (turtle ships), which are believed to be the world's first iron-clad battleships.

On land, volunteer peasant fighters and contingents of Buddhist monks gallantly engaged the enemy. The Japanese began to withdraw from Korea following the death of the warlord Toyotomi Hideyoshi. The war finally ended in 1598, but had a disastrous impact upon both Korea's Joseon Dynasty and Ming China. During the war, numerous Korean artisans and technicians, including potters, were forcibly taken to Japan.

From the early 17th Century, a movement advocating *Silhak*, or practical learning, gained considerable momentum among liberal-minded scholar-officials as a means of building a modern nation.

They strongly recommended agricultural and industrial improvement along with sweeping reforms in land distribution. The conservative government aristocrats, however, were not ready to accommodate such a drastic change.

In the latter half of the Joseon era, government administration and the upper classes came to be marked by recurring factionalism. To rectify the undesirable political situation, King Yeongjo (r. 1724-1776) eventually adopted a policy of impartiality. He was thus able to strengthen the royal authority and achieve political stability.

King Jeongjo (r. 1776-1800) maintained the policy of impartiality and set up a royal library to preserve royal documents and records. He also initiated other political and cultural reforms. This period witnessed the blossoming of *Silhak*. A number of outstanding scholars wrote progressive works recommending agricultural and industrial reforms, but few of their ideas were adopted by the government.

Japanese Occupation and Korea's Independence Movement

In the 19th century, Korea remained a "Hermit Kingdom," adamantly opposed to Western demands for diplomatic and trade relations. Over time, a few Asian and European countries with imperialistic ambitions competed with each other for influence over the Korean Peninsula. Japan, after winning wars

Citizens participating in the Independence Movement against Japanese colonial rule.

against China and Russia, forcibly annexed Korea and instituted colonial rule in 1910.

Colonial rule stimulated the patriotism of Koreans. Korean intellectuals were infuriated by Japan's official assimilation policy, which even banned Korean-language education in Korean schools. On March 1, 1919, Koreans staged nationwide protests during which thousands of lives were lost.

Although it failed, the March 1 Independence Movement created strong bonds of national identity and patriotism among Koreans. The movement led to the establishment of a Provisional Government in Shanghai, China, as well as an organized armed struggle against the Japanese colonialists in Manchuria. The Independence Movement is still commemorated among Koreans every March 1, which is designated a national holiday.

The lives of Koreans deteriorated under colonial rule until Japan's defeat in World War II in 1945. During the colonial period, Japan's economic exploitation of Korea continued.

The Founding of the Republic of Korea

Koreans rejoiced at Japan's World War II defeat. However, their joy was short-lived. Liberation did not instantly bring about the independence for which the Koreans had fought so fiercely.

Rather, it resulted in a country divided by ideological differences caused by the emerging Cold War. Korean efforts to establish an independent government were frustrated as U.S. forces occupied the southern half of the peninsula and the Soviet troops took control of the north.

In November 1947, the United Nations General Assembly adopted a resolution that called for general elections in Korea under the supervision of a U.N. Commission.

However, the Soviet Union refused to comply with the resolution and denied the U.N. Commission access to the northern half of Korea. The U.N. General Assembly then adopted another resolution calling for elections in areas accessible to the U.N. Commission. The first elections in Korea were carried out on May 10, 1948, in the areas south of the 38th parallel. This parallel came to divide the Korean Peninsula into north and south.

Syngman Rhee was elected the first President of the Republic of Korea in 1948. Meanwhile, north of the 38th parallel, a Communist regime was set up under the leadership of Kim Il-sung.

On June 25, 1950, North Korea launched an unprovoked full-scale invasion of the South, triggering a three-year war which was joined by U.S., Chinese and other foreign forces. The entire peninsula was devastated by the conflict. A cease-fire was signed in July 1953.

The war left almost three million Koreans dead or

wounded and millions of others homeless and separated from their families. Serious social disorder continued under the government of President Syngman Rhee.

Korea's democracy was not mature at the time, and the country experienced tremendous political and economic difficulties. President Rhee stepped down in April 1960 as a result of a student-led uprising. The Second Republic was established as Chang Myon of the Democratic Party formed a government in August 1960.

However, the new government was brought down by a coup d'etat led by Major General Park Chunghee on May 16, 1961. The Supreme Council for National Reconstruction headed by General Park took over the legislative, executive, and judicial functions of the government.

Park became President in an election in 1963. Park's government pursued rapid industrialization and achieved high economic growth during the 1960s and 70s, often dubbed "the Miracle on the Hangang River," but his rule was accompanied by severe restriction of people's political rights and civil liberties.

The assassination of President Park in October 1979 brought a transition period under martial law. Choi Kyu-hah, who was installed as a caretaker President, resigned in August 1980, and Chun Doohwan, leader of a powerful officers' group, was elected President by the National Conference for Unification, an electoral college.

Pro-democracy movements intensified throughout the 1980s and presidential election by direct popular vote was restored in a constitutional revision in 1987.

Roh Tae-woo, also a former general, was elected

President under the new Constitution but the democratic advances achieved during his administration set the stage for the election of the first civilian president in 32 years.

Kim Young-sam, a long-time pro-democracy activist, was elected president in 1992 on the ruling party ticket.

In the 1997 presidential election, Kim Dae-jung, leader of the major opposition National Congress for New Politics (NCNP), was elected. His administration, called the "Government of the People," was created through the first-ever peaceful transfer of power from the ruling to an opposition party in Korean constitutional history.

The Roh Moo-hyun administration, or the "Participatory Government," was launched on February 25, 2003. The Roh administration, the 16th in the republic's history, set forth three goals: "Democracy with the People," "Society of Balanced Development," and "Era of Peace and Prosperity in Northeast Asia."

The Roh Moo-hyun government was born by the strength of the people's power. The voluntary fund-raising and election campaigns by those citizens who cherish principles and commonsense led to Roh's victory in the presidential election.

First and foremost, the Roh government was created on the basis of the power of popular participation. As such, popular participation will play a pivotal role in the future operation of the government, as it did during its birth.

Constitution and Government

The Constitution

On July 17, 1948, the first Constitution of the Republic of Korea was adopted. As the nation underwent political upheavals in pursuit of democratic development, the Korean Constitution has been amended nine times, the last time on October 29, 1987.

The current Constitution represents a major advancement in the direction of full democratization. Apart from a legitimate process of revision, a number of substantive changes are notable. They include the curtailment of presidential powers, the strengthening of the power of the legislature and additional devices for the protection of human rights. In particular, the creation of a new, independent Constitutional Court played a vital role in making Korea a more democratic and free society.

The Constitution consists of a preamble, 130 articles, and six supplementary rules. It is divided into 10 chapters: General Provisions, Rights and Duties of Citizens, the National Assembly, the Executive, the Courts, the Constitutional Court, Election Management, Local Authority, the Economy, and Amendments to the Constitution.

The basic principles of the Korean Constitution include the sovereignty of the people, separation of powers, and the pursuit of peaceful and democratic unification of South and North Korea, the pursuit of international peace and cooperation, the rule of law and the responsibility of the state to promote welfare.

The Constitution envisages a liberal democratic political order. It not only declares in its Preamble that the Republic of Korea aims to "further strengthen the basic free and democratic order," but also institutionalizes the separation of powers and the rule of law. The Constitution adopts a presidential system supplemented by parliamentary elements. It provides political parties with constitutional privileges and protection while imposing on them constitutional duties not to impair the free and democratic political order.

In Article 10, the Constitution declares that, "All citizens shall be assured of human worth and dignity and have the right to pursue happiness. It shall be the duty of the State to confirm and guarantee the fundamental and inviolable human rights of individuals." Based on this basic provision, the Constitution provides for individual civil, political and social rights that have become the norm in democratic countries.

They include equality before the law, personal liberty, the right to a speedy and fair trial, freedom of movement, freedom of occupation, the right to privacy, freedom of religion and conscience, freedom of expression and association, the right to participate in political processes such as the right to vote and hold public office.

In addition, the state has to guarantee various social rights ranging from the right to education, and the workers's right to independent association, to collective bargaining and collective action and the right to a healthy and pleasant environment.

The Korean National Flag

The Korean National Flag, *Taegeukgi,* adopted during the latter years of the Joseon Dynasty, takes its name from the *Taegeuk* circle in the center of the flag, which is divided equally and in perfect balance. The upper red section represents *yang* and the blue lower section represents *eum,*

 an ancient symbol of the universe – depicting the powerful cosmic forces that oppose each other but achieve perfect harmony and balance: fire and water, day and night, dark and light, masculine and feminine, heat and cold, positive and negative, and so on.

The trigrams bars at each corner also carry the ideas of opposition and balance. The three unbroken lines stand for heaven; the opposite three broken lines represent earth. At the lower left corner are two lines with a broken line in between, symbolizing fire. Diagonally opposite is the symbol of water. The white background shows the purity of the Korean people and their peace-loving spirit. The flag as a whole symbolizes the ideal of the Korean people of living in harmony with the universe.

Article 37 provides that the fundamental rights of citizens shall not be neglected simply because they are not enumerated in the Constitution. It also prescribes that those rights may be restricted only by law and only when necessary for national security, the maintenance of law and order, or general welfare. Even when such restriction is imposed, no essential aspect of the freedom or right shall be violated.

The Constitution makes it clear that all citizens have basic duties, namely, the duty to pay taxes, the duty to work, and the duty of national defense under the conditions as prescribed by law.

Notable in the current Constitution is the establish-ment of the Constitutional Court as the protector of the Constitution and the guarantor of citizens funda-mental rights.

The Constitution also assumes a free market econ-omy by declaring that the State guarantees the right to property and encourages the freedom and creative initiative of enterprises and individuals in economic affairs. It also provides that the State may regulate and coordinate economic affairs in order to maintain the balanced growth and stability of the national economy, and achieve the democratization of the economy.

Constitutional amendment requires special proce-dures different from other legislation. Either the President or a majority of the National Assembly may submit a proposal for constitutional amendment. An amendment needs the concurrence not only of the National Assembly but also of a national referendum. The former requires support of two-thirds or more of the National Assembly members, while the latter requires more than one half of all votes cast by more than one half of eligible voters in a national referen-dum.

The President

The President of the Republic of Korea, elected by nationwide, equal, direct and secret ballot, stands at the apex of the executive branch.

The President serves a single five-year term, with no additional terms being allowed. This single-term provision is a safeguard for preventing any individual from holding the reins of government power for a protracted period of time. In the event of presidential disability or death, the Prime Minister or members of the State Council will temporarily serve as the President as determined by law.

Under the current political system, the President plays five major roles. First, the President is head of state, symbolizing and representing the entire nation both in the governmental system and in foreign relations.

He receives foreign diplomats, awards decorations and other honors, and grants pardons. He has the duty to safeguard the independence, territorial integrity, and continuity of the state and to uphold the Constitution, in addition to the unique task of pursuing the peaceful reunification of Korea.

Second, the President is the chief administrator, and thus enforces the laws passed by the legislature while issuing orders and decrees for the enforcement of laws. The President has full power to direct the State Council and a varying number of advisory organs and executive agencies. He is authorized to appoint public officials, including the Prime Minister and heads of executive agencies.

Third, the President is commander-in-chief of the armed forces. He has extensive authority over military policy, including the power to declare war.

Fourth, the President is the chief diplomat and foreign policy maker. He accredits or dispatches diplomatic envoys, and signs treaties with foreign nations.

Finally, the President is chief policy maker and a key lawmaker. He may propose legislative bills to the National Assembly or express his views to the legislature in person or in writing. The President cannot dissolve the National Assembly, but the Assembly can hold the President ultimately accountable to the Constitution by means of an impeachment process.

The Executive Branch

Under Korea's presidential system, the President performs his executive functions through the State Council made up of 15 to 30 members and presided over by the President, who is solely responsible for deciding all important government policies. The Prime Minister is appointed by the President and approved by the National Assembly. As the principal executive assistant to the President, the Prime Minister supervises the administrative ministries and manages the Office for Government Policy Coordination under the direction of the President. The Prime Minister also has the power to deliberate major national policies and to attend the meetings of the National Assembly.

Two Deputy Prime Ministers are assigned to carry out the particular affairs delegated by the Prime Minister. Minister of Finance and Economy and Minister of Education and Human Resources Development hold offices of Deputy Prime Minister at the same time.

Members of the State Council are appointed by the President upon recommendation by the Prime Minister. They have the right to lead and supervise their administrative ministries, deliberate major state affairs, act on behalf of the President and appear at the National Assembly and express their opinions. Members of the State Council are collectively and individually responsible to the President only.

In addition to the State Council, the President has several agencies under his direct control to formulate and carry out national policies: the Board of Audit and Inspection, the National Intelligence Service, the Civil Service Commission and the Korea Independent Commission Against Corruption. Heads

Government Structure of the Republic of Korea

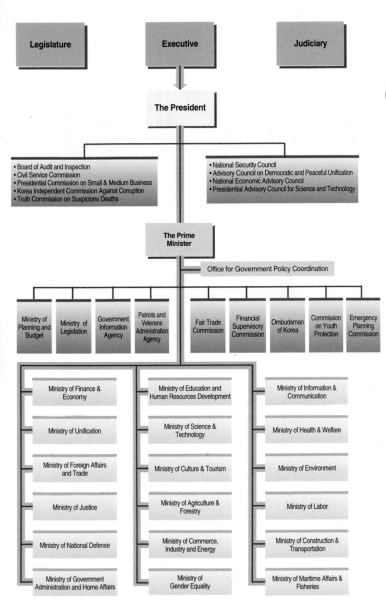

Legislature

Executive

Judiciary

The President

- Board of Audit and Inspection
- Civil Service Commission
- Presidential Commission on Small & Medium Business
- Korea Independent Commission Against Corruption
- Truth Commission on Suspicions Deaths

- National Security Council
- Advisory Council on Democratic and Peaceful Unification
- National Economic Advisory Council
- Presidential Advisory Council for Science and Technology

The Prime Minister

Office for Government Policy Coordination

Ministry of Planning and Budget

Ministry of Legislation

Government Information Agency

Patriots and Veterans Administration Agency

Fair Trade Commission

Financial Supervisory Commission

Ombudsman of Korea

Commission on Youth Protection

Emergency Planning Commission

Ministry of Finance & Economy

Ministry of Education and Human Resources Development

Ministry of Information & Communication

Ministry of Unification

Ministry of Science & Technology

Ministry of Health & Welfare

Ministry of Foreign Affairs and Trade

Ministry of Culture & Tourism

Ministry of Environment

Ministry of Justice

Ministry of Agriculture & Forestry

Ministry of Labor

Ministry of National Defense

Ministry of Commerce, Industry and Energy

Ministry of Construction & Transportation

Ministry of Government Administration and Home Affairs

Ministry of Gender Equality

Ministry of Maritime Affairs & Fisheries

The Central Government Complex on Sejongno

of these organizations are appointed by the President, but the presidential appointment of the Chairman of the Board of Audit and Inspection is subject to the approval of the National Assembly.

The Board of Audit and Inspection has the authority to audit the financial accounts of central and local government agencies, government corporations, and related organizations. The board is also vested with the power to inspect abuses of public authority or misconduct by public officials in their official duties. The results of audit are reported to the President and the National Assembly, although the board is responsible only to the chief executive.

The National Intelligence Service is authorized to collect strategic intelligence of internal as well as external origin and information on subversive and international criminal activities. It also plans and coordinates the intelligence and security activities of the government.

The Civil Service Commission, established in 1999, is responsible for the fair and efficient personnel management of civil servants.

The Korea Independent Commission Against Corruption, established in 2002, has the authority to take all necessary measures to prevent corruption; to design and evaluate anti-corruption policies, to enhance education and public relations and to inspect report and protect whistle-blowers.

Legislature

Legislative power is vested in the National Assembly, a unicameral legislature. The Assembly is composed of 273 members serving a four-year term.

Assembly members elected by popular vote comprise five-sixths of membership with the remaining seats distributed proportionately among parties winning five seats or more in a direct election. The proportional representation system is aimed at appointing Assembly members who will represent national interests rather than local interests.

To be eligible for election, a candidate must be at least 25 years of age. One candidate from each electoral district is selected by a plurality of votes.

An Assembly member is not held responsible outside the Assembly for any opinions expressed or votes cast in the legislative chamber. During a session of the Assembly, no Assembly member may be arrested or detained without consent of the Assembly except in the case of a flagrant criminal act.

In case of apprehension or detention of an Assembly member prior to the opening of a session, the member must be released during the session upon the request of the Assembly.

Two types of legislative sessions are provided for, regular and special. The regular session is convened once a year from September through December and special sessions may be convened upon the request of the President or one-fourth or more of the members of the Assembly. The period of a regular session is limited to 100 days and to 30 days for special sessions. If the President requests the convening of a special session, he must clearly specify the period of the session and the reasons for the request.

Except as otherwise provided in the Constitution or law, the attendance of more than one half of the entire Assembly members, and the concurrent vote of more than one half of the Assembly members present, are necessary to make decisions of the National Assembly binding. In the case of a tie vote, the matter is considered to be rejected by the Assembly. Legislative meetings are open to the public, but this rule may be waived with the approval of more than one half of the members present or when the Speaker deems it necessary to do so in the interest of national security.

The National Assembly is vested with a number of functions under the Constitution, the foremost of which is making laws. Other functions of the Assembly include approval of the national budget, matters related to foreign policy, declaration of war, and the dispatch of armed forces abroad or the stationing of foreign forces within the country; inspecting or investigating specific matters of state affairs; and impeachment.

A motion for impeachment must be proposed by one-third or more of the membership of the Assembly. The vote of a majority of the Assembly is necessary to approve an impeachment motion. However, a motion for the impeachment of the President should be proposed by a majority of the total members of the Assembly, and approved by the

The National Assembly

concurrent vote of two-thirds or more of the entire membership. When an impeachment motion is passed by the National Assembly, the case is sent to the Constitutional Court for trial.

The Assembly elects one Speaker and two Vice Speakers, who serve for two-year terms. The Speaker presides over plenary sessions and represents the legislature while supervising its administration. The Vice Speakers assist the Speaker and take the chair in his absence.

The Standing Committees

The Assembly maintains 16 standing committees with the following functional designations: House Steering; Legislation and Judiciary; National Policy; Finance and Economy; Unification, Foreign Affairs and Trade; National Defense; Government Administration and Local Autonomy; Education; Science, Technology, Information and Telecommunication; Culture and Tourism; Agriculture, Forestry, Maritime Affairs and Fisheries; Commerce, Industry and Energy; Health and Welfare; Environment and Labor; Construction and Transportation; and

Intelligence.

Chairmen of the standing committees are elected from among members of the respective committees. The number of members of a standing committee is determined by Assembly regulations.

The committee chairman is authorized to control the proceedings, maintain order, and represent the committee. Bills and petitions are referred to the standing committees for examination. The committees constitute the primary forum for reconciling differences between the ruling and opposition parties.

Under the present National Assembly Act, each political group having 20 or more Assembly members may form a negotiation group, which acts as a unit in inter-party Assembly negotiations.

Assembly members without party affiliation can form a separate negotiation group if their number is 20 or more. The negotiation groups name floor leaders and whips, who are responsible for negotiating with other groups.

The floor leaders discuss schedules for Assembly sessions and agenda items for plenary and committee meetings.

Judiciary

The Judiciary of Korea consists of three levels of courts: the Supreme Court, High Courts, and District Courts including the specialized Patent Court, Family Court and Administrative Court. The courts exercise jurisdiction over civil, criminal, administrative, electoral, and other judicial matters, while also overseeing affairs related to the registration of real estate, census registers, deposits, and judicial clerks.

The Supreme Court is the highest judicial tribunal. It hears appeals from the decisions rendered by lower courts and court-martial verdicts. The Chief Justice of the Supreme Court is appointed by the President with the consent of the National Assembly. Other justices are appointed by the President upon the recommendation of the Chief Justice. The term of office for the Chief Justice after approval by the National Assembly is six years and a second term is not allowed. The Chief Justice must retire from office at the age of 70. The term for other justices is six years but they may be re-appointed in accordance with the provisions of law, although they must retire from office when they reach the age of 65.

High Courts hear appeals from decisions in civil, criminal and administrative cases rendered by district and family courts and try special cases designated by law.

The Patent Court reviews decisions rendered by the Patent Office as an intermediate appellate jurisdiction. The Supreme Court is the final tribunal over patent disputes.

District Courts are located in Seoul and in the following 12 cities: Incheon, Suwon, Chuncheon, Daejeon, Cheongju, Daegu, Busan, Changwon, Ulsan, Gwangju, Jeonju and Jeju.

The Family Court is empowered to hear all cases involving matrimonial, juvenile, or other domestic matters. The Administrative Court handles administrative cases only.

District Courts outside of Seoul perform the functions of the Administrative Court in their respective districts. In addition to these courts there are military tribunals which exercise jurisdiction over offenses committed by members of the Armed Forces and their civilian employees.

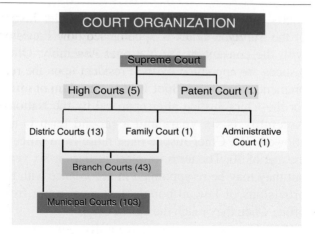

The Constitutional Court

The Constitutional Court was established in September 1988 as a key part of the constitutional system. The Constitution of the Sixth Republic, based on the Korean people's deep enthusiasm for democracy, adopted a new judicial review system – the Constitutional Court– to safeguard the Constitution and to protect the people's basic rights, by establishing special constitutional adjudication procedures for the adjudication of constitutional issues.

The Court is empowered by the Constitution of the Republic of Korea to interpret the Constitution and to review the constitutionality of all statutes, to make judicial decisions on impeachment or on dissolution of a political party, and to pass judgment in competence disputes and constitutional complaints.

The Court is composed of nine Justices. The term of office for Justices is six years and is renewable. The courthouse is a five-story domed building in Seoul which has won the Korean Architectural Award.

As of December 31, 2001, the court has examined

7,389 cases (including 462 cases involving the constitutionality of statutes) and handed down decisions in 6,927 cases, with 462 cases pending.

This high volume of cases shows the Court's present and future significance in implementing its goals- safeguarding the constitution and protecting basic rights.

Local Government

The Constitution of the Republic of Korea states in Article 117 that, "Local governments deal with matters pertaining to the welfare of local residents, manage properties, and may within the limit of laws, enact provisions relating to local autonomy regulations."

The Local Autonomy Act was adopted in 1949, and local councils were operated until 1961 when the military government disbanded them.

Rapid regional development during the 1970s and 1980s, however, strengthened the demand for more autonomous local governments. In order to meet this demand more efficiently, the central government began in the mid-1980s to encourage feasibility studies and to make plans for the resumption of local autonomy.

In 1988, the government initiated a revision of the Local Autonomy Act. According to the new act, Local council elections took place in March 1991, for various *si* (city), *gun* (county), and *gu*(autonomous district) and in June 1991, for metropolitan cities and *do* (provinces). Elections for governors and mayors were held in 1995.

Currently, there are 16 higher-level local governments, including seven metropolitan city governments and nine do governments, and 232 lower-level

local governments including 74 *si* (city) governments, 89 *gun* (county) governments, and 69 *gu*
(autonomous district) governments within the metropolitan cities.

Local government heads manage and supervise
administrative affairs except as otherwise provided
by law. The local executive functions include those
delegated by the central government such as the
management of public properties and facilities and
assessment and collection of local taxes and fees for
various services. Higher-level local governments
have boards of education which carry out matters
related to education and culture in each community.

Higher-level local governments basically serve as
intermediaries between the central and lower-level
local governments.

Lower-level local governments deliver services to
the residents through an administrative district (*eup*,
myeon, and *dong*) system. Each lower-level local
government has several districts which serve as field
offices for handling the needs of their residents. *Eup*,
Myeon, and *Dong* offices are engaged mainly in rou-
tine administrative and social service functions.

Local Governments

Seoul Metropolitan
Area: 606 km²
Population: 10.3 million

Gangwon-do
Area: 16,874 km²
Population: 1.6 million

Busan Metropolitan
Area: 760 km²
Population: 3.8 million

Chungcheongbuk-do
Area: 7,432 km²
Population: 1.5 million

Daegu Metropolitan
DAEGU
Area: 886 km²
Population: 2.5 million

Chungcheongnam-do
Area: 8,586 km²
Population: 1.9 million

Incheon Metropolitan
Area: 965 km²
Population: 2.5 million

Jeollabuk-do
전라북도
Area: 8,050 km²
Population: 2.0 million

Gwangju Metropolitan
Area: 501 km²
Population: 1.4 million

Jeollanam-do
Area: 11,986 km²
Population: 2.1 million

Daejeon Metropolitan
Area: 540 km²
Population: 1.4 million

Gyeongsangbuk-do
Area: 19,024 km²
Population: 2.8 million

Ulsan Metropolitan
ULSAN
Area: 1,056 km²
Population: 1.0 million

Gyeongsangnam-do
Area: 10,515 km²
Population: 3.1 million

Gyeonggi-do
Area: 10,190 km²
Population: 9.2 million

Jeju-do
Area: 1,846 km²
Population: 0.5 million

Inter-Korean Relations

Historical Background

The 1950-53 Korean War not only resulted in a tremendous loss of life and destruction of property, but also left a wide rift among Koreans. After the war, both sides confronted each other across the Demilitarized Zone (DMZ), amidst the tension of the Cold War.

While North Korea pursued Communist unification based on its logic of a so-called "One Joseon (meaning one Korea)," South Korea considered its government as the only legitimate entity on the Korean Peninsula with unification being an extension of its sovereignty. These rigid, uncompromising views made accommodation between the two sides impossible until the 1960s.

However, the international environment became more reconciliatory in the 1970s. The two Koreas recognized each other's government, which marked an epochal change in their attitudes toward reunification. The first positive sign of change came on Liberation Day in 1970 with a call from the South for bona fide peaceful competition with the North.

In August of the following year, South and North Korean Red Cross representatives held the first face-to-face meeting in 26 years since the division. Both governments cooperated with each other in trying to achieve family reunions for those separated during the Korean War.

In 1972, the two governments reached an agreement on principles of unification, and announced the results in the July 4 South-North Joint Communique. Since then, both governments have continued to talk intermittently and had contacts through various channels despite many obstacles.

In 1985, a memorable event resulted from the Red Cross Talks: members of separated families, 50 from each side, visited the other side to find their long-lost relatives. Other notable events were the South-North Economic Talks (1984) and preliminary conferences for South-North National Assembly Talks (1985). Unfortunately, these additional channels of talks between the South and the North were suspended for various political reasons.

In the 1990s, rapid changes occurred in Socialist bloc countries, which politically influenced the Korean Peninsula. Of note, in 1990, the South-North High Level Talks between the Prime Ministers from both sides started and in 1991 produced the "South-North Basic Agreement." It recognized that the South and North were in a "temporary special relationship" in the process toward reunification.

The "Joint Declaration of Denuclearization" was signed and took effect as of February 1992. However, even before the "South-North Basic Agreement" could bear tangible fruit, North Korea's attempt to arm itself with nuclear weapons revived tensions on the Korean Peninsula.

To ease and break through the tension by building mutual trust, the two Koreas agreed in July 1994 to hold summit talks between South Korean President Kim Young-sam and North Korean leader Kim Il-sung. But the sudden death of Kim Il-sung ended this effort.

The Administration of President Kim Dae-jung (1998-2002) ushered in another era of reconciliation and cooperation with North Korea. Underscoring his "Sunshine Policy," President Kim visited Pyongyang in 2000 to hold the first-ever summit with his North Korean counterpart, Kim Jong-il. The historic June 15 Joint Declaration was signed emphasizing the promotion of mutual understanding, developing inter-Korean relations, and achieving peaceful reunification. Projects of mutual interests were discussed and reunions of separated families have been held in Seoul and Pyongyang.

President Kim Dae-jung received the 2000 Nobel Peace Prize in recognition of his years of struggle to improve democracy and human rights in his native land and his efforts for reconciliation between South and North Korea.

Inter-Korean Exchanges and Cooperation

Trade between South and North Korea was legalized in South Korea by the July 7 Special Declaration of 1988. In 2002, trade between the two Koreas reached US$641.73 million.

Based on a policy of separating economics from politics, South Korea introduced a measure to expand inter-Korean economic cooperation on April 30, 1998. Seoul now allows executives of major business companies as well as economic organizations to visit North Korea for business purposes.

In the area of trade and business ventures, the government has increased the number of goods for import on a blanket approval basis while reducing the number of items that require prior approval from 205 to 186. The government also eased restrictions on shipments to North Korea of manufacturing facili-

Inter-Korean Trade (1998-2002)

(unit:US$1,000)

year	Imports from North	Exports to North	Total
1998	92,264	129,679	221,943
1999	121,604	211,832	333,437
2000	152,373	272,775	425,148
2001	176,170	226,787	402,957
2002	271,575	370,155	641,730

ties for the production of goods by South Korean enterprises in North Korea and eased restrictions on the amount of investment allowed in the North.

While maintaining a strong national security system, the government will steadily expand inter-Korean economic cooperation as relations between the South and North continue to improve.

Inter-Korean trade in 2002 recorded at $641.7 million, up 59.3 percent from a year earlier. A total of $271.5 million worth of merchandise was shipped from North Korea to South Korea, a 54.2 percent increase, while $370.1 million worth of goods were sent to the North, a 63.2 percent surge. A bulk of North Korean exports includes agricultural, fishery, and textile products. Major South Korean goods were chemical industrial and textile products. Cargo and cruise operations between North and South Korea totaled 1,827 in 2002, up 8.4 percent from the previous year. Inter-Korean shipping, on the other hand, posted 1.09 million metric tons, 70.2 percent up.

The Roh Moo-hyun Administration's Policy of Inter-Korean Reconciliation and Cooperation

The Roh Moo-hyun government is broadening the horizon and looking at inter-Korean reconciliation

President Roh Moo-hyun is taking the oath of office during his inauguration on February 25, 2003.

and cooperation as well as peace on the Korean Peninsula. If there were an absence of peace on the Korean Peninsula, it wouldn't be possible to expect progress of the nation or even peace and prosperity of Northeast Asia to develop.

In the past few years, efforts at peace have increased with much progress. Through the inter-Korean summit meeting held in June 2000, the two Koreas paved a path toward resolving the unification issue through dialogue and cooperation. It also provided an impetus for the two Koreas to resolve a confrontation that was one of the causes of instability in Northeast Asia.

In late 2002, North Korea admitted that it had been conducting a major nuclear-weapons development program for the past several years. South Korea urged North Korea to abide by a series of agreements it now clearly violates: the Nuclear Nonproliferation

Buses bound for Mt. Geumgangsan in North Korea are embarking on their first-ever overland trip on February 23, 2003.

Treaty, the 1994 agreement, and a joint declaration signed with South Korea to keep the Korean peninsula nuclear-free.

The Roh government is seeking to build a structure of peace on the Korean Peninsula with the institutionalization of peace through the improvement of inter Korean relations. The government's plan states that all the issues including the North's nuclear program should be resolved through peaceful methods and by dialogue. Inter-Korean reconciliation and cooperation and persuading North Korea to participate in the international community must be consistently promoted.

The government will regularize inter-Korean talks including summit meetings. Under the principle of "Priority on Mutual Trust," the government will focus on increasing trust between the South and the North by firmly establishing the practice of carrying out mutually agreed matters.

The Roh administration will broaden and deepen inter-Korean exchange and cooperation. South Korea will lay a foundation for a prosperous community through the expansion and development of inter-Korean economic cooperation projects and focus on restoring national homogeneity by expanding social and cultural exchanges.

Korea in the World

Korea's International Relations

Since its founding in 1948, the Republic of Korea has been committed to the concepts of democracy and a free-market economy, but its foreign relations have undergone significant changes since its founding. As the East-West confrontation centered around the United States and the USSR evolved into a state of Cold War following World War II, the Republic of Korea pursued its foreign relations in concert with the nations of the West, who advocated democracy. In the years following the Korean War (1950-53), the international community viewed Korea as a devastated, poverty-ridden state. But that image began to change in 1962 when the Republic of Korea adopted a policy of export-driven economic development and began to actively pursue international commerce worldwide.

As the East-West confrontation sharpened during the Cold War, the Republic of Korea, regarded as a member of the Western bloc, began to expand its foreign relations by improving ties with traditional allies and by building cooperative relations with Third-World nations. Since the 1970s, the diplomacy of the Republic of Korea has been designed to promote the independent and peaceful reunification of the peninsula. The ROK has also fortified its ties with allies and actively participated in international organizations.

With its diplomatic foundation firmly in place, the Republic of Korea continued throughout the 1980s to pursue cooperative partnerships with all countries in every field. In the late 1980s and early 1990s, epochal changes in Eastern Europe and the Soviet Union brought an end to the Cold War, while the Republic of Korea moved swiftly to exploit the situation by actively promoting a "Northern Diplomacy."

Korea's energetic pursuit of the Northern Diplomacy contributed to the enhancing of its ties with former socialist countries, with whom relations had languished due to ideological and structural differences. Relations with most such countries, including the Soviet Union and China, were normalized in short order, thus enabling Korea's foreign relations to become truly global. South and North Korea joined the United Nations simultaneously in September 1991, crowning the success of the Northern Diplomacy.

Furthermore, the foundation for peaceful coexistence between the South and North was laid in December 1991, when they concluded the Agreement on Reconciliation, Nonaggression and Exchanges and Cooperation (the Basic South-North Agreement) and the Joint Declaration of the Denuclearization of the Korean Peninsula.

These historic documents planted the seeds of peace on the peninsula and in Northeast Asia, representing an important first step toward the peaceful reunification of the divided nation.

Korea's International Economic Relations

In the wake of the Cold War, a distinct trend toward regionalism emerged. Countries like the Republic of Korea, which have pursued export-led growth, found themselves facing a different international economic environment than in the past. Korea has mostly traded with advanced countries —the United States, Japan and the European Union.

This has often caused friction over trade imbalances. As Korea has gradually increased its trade with developing countries, however, the share of its trade with advanced countries has steadily declined.

The Republic of Korea's trade with developing countries and the nations of Eastern Europe will continue to expand as long as Korea's economy and trade continue to grow and the nation's industrial structure continues to focus on technology-intensive activities. Once Korea has completed its industrial restructuring, it will be able to make a greater contribution to international economic development by accelerating cooperation with developing countries on the basis of its comparative advantages and complementarity.

To the extent that advanced countries remain key to trade and crucial as partners in industrial science and technology, Korea will have to endeavor to minimize friction by opening its markets to a similar extent that the developed countries markets are open, starting with industrial goods and agricultural products and including services as well.

Global environmental issues, such as depletion of the ozone layer, global warming and deforestation, have emerged as new challenges to people throughout the world.

The June 1992 United Nations Conference on Environment and Development (UNCED) - known as the Earth Summit - drove home to Korea the message that continuous economic development must not be allowed to harm the environment that sustains us all. Koreans were particularly proud of their contribution to the adoption of the Rio Declaration and Agenda 21. The aim of the new policy is to seek reconciliation between the environment and economic development, a balance between trade and the environment, and active participation in global efforts for environmental protection.

The Uruguay Round basically provided for a comprehensive reduction in tariffs and a general removal of non-tariff trade barriers, a crucial step in the global movement toward free trade. The Republic of Korea proactively opens its market to support a global free trade system.

Diplomatic Activities for International Peace and Cooperation

The Republic of Korea joined the United Nations(UN) in September 1991, expanding its active participation and contribution in multilateral diplomacy commensurate with its elevated stature in the global community. In September 2001, Dr. Han Seung-soo, then Minister of Foreign Affairs and Trade, was elected by acclamation as President of the 56th Session of the General Assembly.

Even before joining the UN, however, the Republic of Korea was active in the United Nations specialized agencies, such as the International Monetary Fund (IMF), the International Bank for Reconstruction and Development (IBRD), the United Nations Industrial Development Organization (UNIDO) and the United Nations Educational, Scientific and Cultural Organization (UNESCO), as well as the General Agreement on Tariffs and Trade (GATT) and other key inter-governmental bodies.

It has also helped to launch the Goodwill

Technicians from developing countries visit Korea to learn about its industrial development and new technologies.

Ambassadors Program adopted by the UN International Drug Control Program as part of activities for the UN Decade Against Drug Abuse. Korea hosted the 18th session of the Meeting of Heads of National Drug Law Enforcement Agencies, Asia and the Pacific, in Seoul in September 1993.

As a member of the UN, the Republic of Korea stepped up efforts to expand its global role. In 1992, the nation became a member of several important UN bodies, such as the Commission on Crime Prevention and Criminal Justice, the Governing Council of the United Nations Development Program (UNDP), the Commission on Human Rights and the Committee for Program and Coordination. At the 47th session of the General Assembly in October 1992, the Republic of Korea was elected to the UN Economic and Social Council, one of the principal UN organs, along with the Security Council and the General Assembly. Korea's financial contribution to the UN regular budget, amounting to US$21 million in 2002, ranks 10th among all member states.

At the Economic and Social Council (ECOSOC) session in January 1993, the Republic of Korea was elected a vice-president, and also became the chairman of the ECOSOC Committee. The Republic of Korea was also elected to the Commission on Sustainable Development, a new commission established under the ECOSOC in February 1993 to coordinate and monitor the activities in the areas of environment and development.

Throughout its decade-long membership in the UN, the Republic of Korea has participated actively in major issues handled by the world body such as conflict prevention and peacekeeping missions, disarmament talks, environmental protection, development projects and human rights protection. In particular, their role as a non-permanent member in the Security Council during the 1996-97 period provided invaluable experience through which Korea broadened its diplomatic profile. During its tenure, Korea contributed constructively in the discussions to address major regional conflicts by highlighting the problem of "political refugees."

As a peace-loving member of the UN, Korea is committed to the maintenance of international peace and security, and is therefore actively participating in UN peacekeeping activities. Korea began by deploying a 250-personnel engineer corps to Somalia (UNOSOM II) in 1993. Since then, it deployed a 42-personnel medical unit to Western Sahara (MINURSO) in 1994 and an engineer corps of 198 personnel to Angola (UNAVEM III) in 1995. Korea has further strengthened its role in peacekeeping activities by deploying for the first time a combat infantry unit of over 400 personnel to East Timor (UNTAET). Furthermore in 2002, a Korean military officer was appointed commander of the UN peacekeeping force in Cyprus (UNFICYP).

Developing countries often face serious problems because they lack experience in preparing economic plans, procuring necessary investment capital and executing the economic policies necessary for sustained economic growth. The Republic of Korea's developmental experience, therefore, can be a model for such nations.

Korea had begun to assist developing countries already in the 1960s, when it invited small numbers of trainees and dispatched a few experts overseas. After 1975, when its economy had reached a higher level, Korea began to increase its assistance in a variety of forms: grants of machinery and materials, construction technology aid, Economic Development Cooperation Fund (EDCF) loans and direct personnel assistance, especially through a Youth Volunteer Program.

The Republic of Korea also provided assistance to developing countries through multilateral organizations such as the IMF, IBRD, ADB and nearly a dozen other international financial organizations.

In April 1991, the Republic of Korea created the Korea International Cooperation Agency (KOICA) under the Ministry of Foreign Affairs to consolidate its assistance to developing countries. It provides technical and financial aid to developing countries and shares Korea's development experience and expertise.

KOICA implements various cooperation programs such as dispatching medical doctors, industry experts, *taekwondo* instructors and other volunteers, inviting trainees to Korea and assisting non-governmental organizations. KOICA contributes to enhancing Korea's image through establishing cooperative relationships with developing countries. Korea contributed US$264 million in Official Development Aid (ODA) in 2001.

The Republic of Korea is committed to the pursuit of cultural exchanges with foreign countries to enhance bilateral friendship and understanding and to contribute to global reconciliation and cooperation. The nation also seeks to introduce Korean traditional art and culture abroad, and supports overseas Korean studies programs as well as numerous academic conferences and athletic exchanges. The Korea Foundation, established in 1991, coordinates and supports international cultural exchange programs.

The Roh Moo-hyun Administration's Policy for Peace and Prosperity in Northeast Asia

The age of Northeast Asia is arriving amid the currents of post-Cold War, globalization, knowledge and information. Northeast Asia today is playing the engine's role for the world economy as capital, technology, production and logistics converge on this region.

The Korean Peninsula, located at the heart of Northeast Asia, is still locked in the Cold War order. The historic structure of conflict among China, Japan, Russia and the United States has yet to see a transformation into a forward-looking system of peace and cooperation.

The Roh Moo-hyun government is seeking to take the initiative in leading Northeast Asia to an era of peace and prosperity. It is crucial for Korea to establish a structure of peace on the Korean Peninsula and build Korea as the hub of Northeast Asia.

The Roh government is also seeking to develop Korea into the economic hub of Northeast Asia by: 1) pursuing inter-Korean economic exchange and cooperation, 2) establishing a system of Northeast Asian economic cooperation, and 3) building infrastructure for a logistics and business hub.

The government plans to build the logistics hub in Northeast Asian through the following steps: 1) developing the Incheon Inter-national Airport as a hub airport of Northeast Asia, while promoting Gwangyang and Busan ports into hub ports of the region, 2) developing the Incheon International Airport and Incheon Port as the logistics hub of the Greater Seoul Metropolitan Area, 3) reconnecting the two inter-Korean railways and roads under construction, and establish a transportation network connecting with the Trans-Siberia Railway (TSR) and the Trans-China Railway (TCR), 4) building an integrated logistics information network linking the airports and ports by 2015.

Economy

Economic Growth

Korea recently pulled through an economic storm that began in late-1997. This crisis, which roiled markets all across Asia, had threatened Korea's remarkable economic achievements. However, thanks to the faithful implementation of an IMF agreement the Korean government's strong resolve for reform, and successful negotiation of foreign debt restructuring with creditor banks, the nation is currently on track to resume economic growth. Since the onset of the crisis, Korea has been rapidly integrating itself into the world economy. The goal of the nation is to overcome problems rooted in the past by creating an economic structure suitable for an advanced economy.

Korea, once known to be one of the world's poorest agrarian societies, has undertaken economic development in earnest since 1962. In less than four decades, it achieved what has become known as the "economic miracle on the Hangang River" a reference to the river that runs through Seoul—an incredible process that dramatically transformed the Korean economy while marking a turning point in Korea's history.

An outward-oriented economic development strategy, which used exports as the engine of growth, contributed greatly to the radical economic transformation of Korea. Based on such a strategy, many

Gross National Income

(in US$ billion)

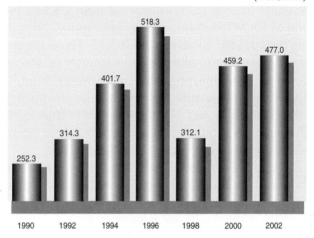

Year	Value
1990	252.3
1992	314.3
1994	401.7
1996	518.3
1998	312.1
2000	459.2
2002	477.0

Per Capita GNI

(in US$)

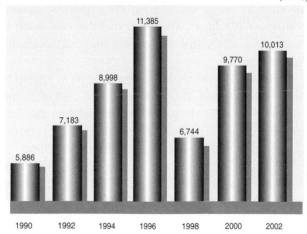

Year	Value
1990	5,886
1992	7,183
1994	8,998
1996	11,385
1998	6,744
2000	9,770
2002	10,013

<Source: The Bank of Korea>

successful development programs were implemented. As a result, from 1962 to 2002, Korea's Gross National Income (GNI) increased from US$2.3 billion to US$477 billion, with its per capita GNI soaring from US$87 to about US$10,013. These impressive figures clearly indicate the magnitude of success that these economic programs have brought about.

GNI and per capita GNI drastically dropped to US$312 billion and US$6,744 in 1998 due to the fluctuation in foreign exchange rates but these figures returned to the pre-economic crisis level in 2002.

Korean imports have steadily increased thanks to the nation's liberalization policy and increasing per capita income levels. As one of the largest import markets in the world, the volume of Korea's imports exceeded those of China in 1995, and were comparable to the imports of Malaysia, Indonesia, and the Philippines combined.

Major import items included industrial raw materials such as crude oil and natural minerals, general consumer products, foodstuffs and goods such as machinery, electronic equipment and transportation equipment.

Korea developed rapidly from the 1960s, fueled by high savings and investment rates, and a strong emphasis on education. The nation became the 29th member country of the Organization for Economic Cooperation and Development (OECD) in 1996.

With a history as one of the fastest growing economies in the world, Korea is working to become the focal point of a powerful Asian economic bloc during the 21st century. The Northeast Asian region commands a superior pool of essential resources that are the necessary ingredients for economic development. These include a population of 1.5 billion peo-

Overall Exports and Imports

(in US$ million)

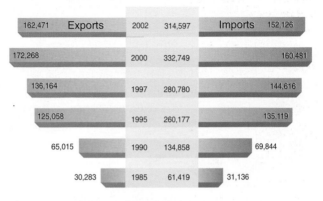

	Exports		Imports	
162,471	Exports	2002	314,597	Imports	152,126
172,268		2000	332,749		160,481
136,164		1997	280,780		144,616
125,058		1995	260,177		135,119
65,015		1990	134,858		69,844
30,283		1985	61,419		31,136

<Source: Ministry of Finance and Economy>

ple, abundant natural resources, and large-scale consumer markets.

Industrial Development

The Korean government is taking major initiatives to improve the nation's economic competitiveness by adopting a floating exchange rate system making available short-term export financing, simplifying customs procedures, and encouraging foreign investment.

Korea's First Five-Year Economic Development Plan (1962-1966) focused on laying a foundation for industrialization. The plan successfully initiated, and then accelerated, a structural adjustment of the nation's industrial structure from subsistence agriculture to modern manufacturing and export trade. In the process of its economic growth, Korea has carried out comprehensive industrialization.

The share of primary industries in the overall

Korea ranked sixth in the world's automobile industry, producing 3 million units in 2002.

industrial structure decreased steadily from 31.5 percent in 1970, to 15.7 percent in 1980, and further to 5 percent in 2002. On the other hand, the share of manufacturing industries increased from 14.7 percent in 1970, to 36.0 percent in 2002.

The share of the service industries stood at 47.5 percent in 2002, by far the leading growth sector in the economy.

Korea's economic growth was initially led by labor-intensive light industries, especially textiles. The light industries were steadily replaced by the heavy and chemical industries that have come to account for over half of the nation's total manufacturing output. For instance, with the completion of the third Gwangyang blast furnace in December 1990, Korea became a major steel producer in the world.

Korea also produces a wide range of industrial

Principal Manufacturing Products

Year	Auto manufacturing (In thousands)	Shipbuilding orders (1,000 Gross/Tonnage)	Steel manufacturing (1,000 Metric/Tonnage)
1970	29	-	1,310
1980	123	1,690	9,341
1990	1,322	4,382	24,868
1995	2,530	7,133	36,772
1997	2,818	12,749	42,554
1999	2,843	11,843	41,042
2000	3,115	20,686	43,107
2002	3,148	9,755	51,983

<Source: Ministry of Commerce, Industry and Energy>

machinery and equipment. The nation's shipbuilding and auto manufacturing industries have reached their peak, while its electronics industry is the leading growth sector and an increasingly important generator of foreign exchange.

Korea is ranked the sixth-largest auto manufacturer in the world, with a production of over 3 million vehicles annually. To meet ever-increasing fuel demand, large petrochemical complexes, supported by several large refineries, have been developed along the coasts of the country.

Other principal industrial products include cement, processed foods, plywood, chemical fertilizers, footwear, clothing, ceramics, glass, nonferrous metals, and farm implements.

In line with the advancement of the nation's industrial structure over recent years, Korea has continued to increase its investment in the manufacturing sector. In particular, government and corporate investment in information and communications technology has been increasing.

Construction-related investment has grown with government support through infrastructure expansion

The shipbuilding industry is the leading growth sector of the Korean economy.

projects, such as railways, roadways, marine ports and airport facilities. This government-led investment is combined with private sector demand for construction of new housing, office buildings and factories.

In 2002, consumer prices in Korea posted a 2.7 percent increase, while producers' prices rose 1.6 percent. During the early 1990s, consumer prices recorded eight to nine percent inflation levels. However, thanks to government efforts to contain inflation as well as improvement in the distribution structure of farm and fisheries products, inflation has decreased considerably.

Korea's overall agricultural production doubled over the last 15 years. Although agricultural growth has since slowed, the much-emphasized goal of self-sufficiency in rice, the staple food of Korea, was attained with an output of 4.9 million tons in 2002.

Agricultural development efforts have been concentrated mainly on maximizing yields from the country's limited arable land, which comprises only about 19 percent of total land area. New high-yield varieties of rice and other crops have been introduced. Also, a large-scale fertilizer and pesticide industry has been developed to keep farmers adequately supplied with these essential products.

There has also been rapid growth in the production of fruits, vegetables and other high-value cash crops, as well as livestock products. The spread of vinyl greenhouses greatly contributed to the increased volume of the nation's vegetable harvest.

The process of industrialization resulted in a steady decrease in Korea's farm population. The ratio of rural residents to the overall population plunged from 57 percent in 1962 to below 9 percent in the late 2000s. This trend has also affected the employment structure of the nation's industry. To solve the problem of rapidly dwindling rural labor, major efforts have been undertaken to promote farm mechanization. Mechanization has progressed significantly in the planting and harvesting of rice.

A nationwide reforestation program has been underway since the early 1970s. The program consists of planting new trees and protecting existing forest areas in the hills of the country, which account for some 64 percent of Korea's land area. Also, new varieties of trees that are more productive and resistant to pests and disease are being developed.

To conserve forestry resources until they become fully productive, tree cutting is strictly controlled. For over a decade, timber production has been limited to around 1,500,000 cubic meters. Most domestic timber demand has thus been satisfied by imports. As an added benefit, these efforts have greatly contributed to the control of flood and soil erosion.

The expansion and modernization of Korea's fishing industry has been remarkable over the past two decades, making it an important source of foreign exchange earnings. The amount of fish harvested has increased rapidly as modern, motorized vessels began to operate in coastal waters as well as the open seas. Korean fishing bases have been established in Western Samoa, Las Palmas and other locations, while consumers now enjoy cuttlefish caught in waters off the Falkland Islands.

Korea's deep-sea catch reached a peak in the mid-1970s and then declined sharply due to rising fuel costs and the declaration of a 200-mile economic sea zones by many nations. Korea has negotiated fishing agreements with a number of coastal nations to secure fishing rights in their territorial waters and is continuing efforts to reinforce its deep-sea fishing industry.

Science and Technology

To reinvigorate the development of advanced science and technology, the government established the Korea Institute of Science and Technology (KIST) and the Ministry of Science and Technology (MOST) in 1966 and 1967, respectively.

Initially, Korea's national science and technology policies focused mainly on the introduction, absorption, and application of foreign technologies. In the 1980s, however, the emphasis shifted to the planning and conducting of national R&D projects to raise the level of scientific and technological skills. This included programs to increase both public and private sector R&D investment, and to nurture highly

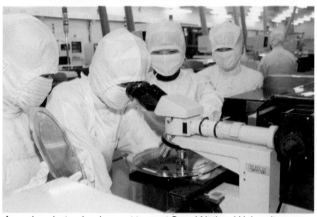

A semiconductor development team at Seoul National University

skilled R&D manpower.

Since the early 1990s the government has been concentrating on three areas: the fostering of research in the basic sciences, securing an efficient distribution and use of R&D resources, and expanding international cooperation. These efforts are intended to increase Korea's technological competitiveness.

With this goal in mind, the Presidential Advisory Council for Science and Technology (PACST) was established in April 1999, to strengthen the overall coordination of national science and technology policy. Its main role is to coordinate major policies and overall plans for promoting science and technology (S&T), expand the science and technology-related investment and set priority for national R&D programs. PACST consists of 19 members including the President as chairman and major cabinet members related to science and technology. In setting up the PACST, the government has been seeking to enhance R&D investment in an effort to develop advanced technologies in the fields of bio-technology, environmental technology, new materials, information technology, and nuclear energy.

Under a "Long-term Plan for National Science and Technology Development," formulated in 1999, Korea envisions to become one of the top seven technologically advanced nations in the world during the first quarter of the 21st century.

As of the end of 2001, Korea's total R&D investment reached US$12.5 billion, which accounted for 2.96 percent of GDP. Korea will also actively invest in the development of public welfare technologies that improve the quality of life and of technologies that can lead to the creation of new industries.

In addition, Korea will continue to strengthen its involvement in global issues such as the preservation of the environment, and a stable supply of food, energy, and health care for the betterment of mankind.

Economic Challenges

Over the past three decades, Korea has enjoyed an annual average economic growth rate of 8.6 percent and has emerged as the world's 12th largest trading nation. In less than two generations, the nation has established itself as one of the world's leading shipbuilders and manufacturers of electronics, semiconductors, and automobiles.

International financial markets positively regarded Korea's economic achievements, including sustained high growth, moderate inflation, high national savings, nominal external deficits, and significant government budget surpluses. Recently, however, these impressive accomplishments have been overshadowed by the difficulties of several major conglomerates and financial institutions. These failures raised doubts among foreign investors, which led to a serious liquidity crisis in late 1997. The crisis also created a serious unemployment problem.

However, following the change of government in 1998, Korea renewed its resolve to work with the IMF to fully implement comprehensive reform measures. As such, Korea was determined to adopt stringent adjustment measures to overcome the economic crisis.

The new leadership took steps to promote reform in the financial, corporate, public and labor sectors with a view to restoring and strengthening foreign investors' confidence as well as maintaining a commitment to a free-market economy, restructuring of the *jaebeol*-based system, and increasing flexibility in the labor market.

The nation's foreign currency reserves that totaled a mere US$3.8 billion as of the end of 1997 rose to $121 billion as of the end of 2002 and the nation has been able to repay all the US$13.5 billion rescue loan from the International Monetary Fund (IMF). The IMF Executive Board on December 16, 1999 declared that the foreign exchange crisis in the Republic of Korea was completely resolved. Korea's credit rating, meanwhile, was restored to investment grade.

Financial Restructuring

A modern, market-based economy cannot function efficiently without dynamic and well-supervised financial institutions. The Financial Supervisory Commission (FSC), which serves as a regulatory mechanism to establish universal banking practices, has created a new system of prudent regulations and supervision, as well as a schedule for reform implementation.

In the process of financial sector reform, the gov-

Korean Stock Exchange

ernment has closed a number of non-viable financial institutions. Other viable banks are following through on the strong remedial actions imposed by the FSC to further improve their soundness. Korea's non-bank financial sector also underwent restructuring. Four insolvent life insurance firms were suspended and will be ultimately taken over by other insurers. A total of 640 non-bank financial firms were suspended or had their licenses revoked.

Korea's government has mobilized fiscal resources totaling 159.0 trillion won (approximately US$134 billion) to support viable financial institutions in regard to their re-capitalization and the disposal of non-performing loans and resolve non-viable financial institutions. The financial institutions have also intensified their own rehabilitation efforts, including downsizing and the inducement of foreign capital investment.

Corporate Restructuring

In the corporate sector, overall results of restructuring have been quite positive. The debt-equity ratio of the manufacturing sector has improved dramatically, from 396% in late 1997 to 130% in September 2002. And the 'too-big-to-fail' myth disappeared while 16 of the 30 largest conglomerates were sold, merged, and liquidated. Rule setting for transparent and responsible management has been carried out and reinforced through the appointment of outside directors, the introduction of audit committees, and the obligatory publication of combined financial statements.

Corporate restructuring of weak companies has been rapidly pursued under the initiative of creditor banks. For example, Dawoo Motors and Hanbo Steel were successfully acquired by foreign capitals. Since the introduction of the work-out program, many financially troubled companies have been normalized.

Progress of work-out procedure

- A total of 83 companies have gone through the program.
- By March 2002, 55 companies successfully completed the program, and 17 companies were promptly liquidated.
- Now 11 remaining firms are in the progress of implementing the program.

The Corporate Restructuring Promotion Act was enacted in September 2001 to expedite prompt and transparent corporate restructuring. In addition, the Constant Corporate Restructuring System has been under way since March 2001, which allows each creditor bank to periodically evaluate the credit risk of debtor companies. The Consolidated Insolvency Law will take effect in the near future.

The purpose of corporate reform is to enhance the

productivity and growth potential of the Korean economy by establishing an efficient and fair market.

Corporate structural reform will continue based on the following principles. First, to enhance management and accounting transparency, it is necessary to focus on constructing a market-friendly oversight system, gaining the trust of market participants. Second, corporate reform should be pursued consistently. Until management transparency meets global standards, corporate restructuring should be promoted on an on-going basis.

Steps to bolster transparency and soundness of corporate governance will be carried out and reinforced. The Management monitoring system will be strengthened within and without the companies by enhancing the role of the audit committee, the board of directors and the rights of minority shareholders and the board of directors. To root out illegal practices such as window dressing and stock price manipulation, class action lawsuits for the securities sector will be allowed in the near future.

The regulations of large conglomerates should work in due course. The ceiling on total equity investment, and regulation of cross-share holdings and debt guarantees will be maintained to help prevent the abuse of management power by majority shareholders and the group owner.

Other Measures

As for the public sector, public institutions and associations have been streamlined and their organizational structures changed. Also, state-owned enterprises are being privatized or have undergone drastic management reform, depending on their business orientation.

To form a consensus on labor-related issues, on February 6, 1998, a Tripartite Committee was formed between representatives from labor, business, and the government. The committee established a framework for an equitable sharing of both economic and non-economic costs, and attained public consensus for the restructuring efforts.

The committee reached an accord that contained a number of measures designed to enhance corporate governed transparency. These measures will also increase unemployment benefits and labor market flexibility.

As a result of the efforts of the Tripartite Committee, the Labor Standards Act (LSA) was revised to allow for more management flexibility when dealing with labor issues. In addition, legislation allowing the establishment of manpower dispatch businesses was put into effect in July 1998.

This business has helped companies enhance the effectiveness of their administrative resources and realize increased cost-savings.

The government has increased labor market flexibility by strictly enforcing legal standards with regard to any illegal strikes or labor practices.

Environment for Foreign Investment

In the early 1960s, Korea strictly screened FDI, confining to selected industries and also restricted the repatriation of capital. However, as economic conditions and the environment of the global and domestic economy changed, the government enacted a liberalized foreign investment law in 1984.

Under the new law, Foreign Direct Investment (FDI) flow into Korea increased steadily from 1984.

In 1993, to make the nation more attractive to for-

Foreign Direct Investment (FDI)

(unit: US$ million)

Year	Total	United States	Japan	Others				
				Total	Hong Kong	Germany	United Kingdom	France
1980	143.1	70.6	42.5	30.0	0.5	8.6	2.3	-
1985	532.2	108.0	364.3	59.9	13.4	11.3	12.3	5.1
1990	802.6	317.5	235.9	249.2	3.0	62.3	44.8	22.4
1995	1,947.2	644.9	418.3	878.2	58.0	44.6	86.7	35.2
1997	6,970.9	3,189.6	265.7	3,515.6	84.6	398.1	258.6	410.7
1998	8,852.6	2,976.0	503.0	5,373.0	38.4	786.8	60.0	367.5
1999	15,541.5	3,739.0	1,750.0	10,052.0	461.0	960.0	479.0	760.0
2000	15,216.7	2,922.0	2,448.0	10,327.0	123.0	1,599.0	84.0	607.0
2001	11,291.8	3,890.0	772.0	7,208.0	167.0	459.0	432.0	426.0
2002	9,101.0	4,500.0	1,403.0	3,198.0	234.0	284.0	115.0	111.0

<Source: Ministry of Commerce, Industry and Energy>

eign investment, the government devised a five-year plan for opening up the domestic market. Entrance to OECD in 1996 stimulated a sharp rise in FDI a year later in 1997, as 57 industries, by far the largest number ever, were fully opened to foreign investors.

The Act on Foreign Investment and Foreign Capital Promotion, revised in the first quarter of 1998, created an almost fully liberalized manufacturing sector.

Active foreign participation is of critical importance to the Korean economy, not only with respect to overcoming the Asian financial crisis in 1997 but more importantly for ensuring long-term, sustainable growth.

The government is committed to creating a favorable environment for foreign investment. Its policy initiatives are focused on facilitating FDI through equity participation and mergers and acquisitions activities involving Korean companies. FDI totaled US$15.2 billion in 2000 and US$11.2 billion in

2001. In 2002, due to the global recession's devastating impact on the Information Technology (IT) sector, FDI into Korea slipped to US$9.1 billion.

The Foreign Exchange Management Act was replaced by the new Foreign Exchange Transaction Act in September 1998. The liberalization measures in the new law were put into effect in two stages by the end of the year 2000. The primary objectives of the new law included the liberalization of the capital account and the further development of the domestic foreign exchange market.

Major items of the First Stage Liberalization included the introduction of a "Negative List System," which is more flexible than the former positive list system. It also liberalized capital account transactions related to business activities with financial institutions, including short-term borrowing from abroad. Authorization of foreign exchange transactions to allow financial institutions to meet certain requirements was another market liberalization effort by the government.

Major items of the Second Stage Liberalization included capital account transactions that remained restricted in the first stage, except for those related to national security and prevention of criminal activities. It allows non-residents to invest in won-denominated domestic deposits with maturities of less than one year as well as allow resident individuals to invest in foreign-currency denominated overseas deposits and securities.

These liberalization measures, however, are not without risks. Therefore, in tandem with their implementation, the government is strengthening oversight regulations and market monitoring, as well as building an early warning system.

Capital Market Liberalization

Korea's strategy for capital market development centers on two interrelated policy initiatives, namely market liberalization and market augmentation. Capital market liberalization will directly increase Korea's access to foreign capital and technology, while market augmentation will improve the operational efficiency of the capital market.

Significant progress has already been realized in the implementation of measures to further open the Korean capital market and reduce barriers to portfolio and direct investment. Foreign investment will be fully liberalized for all industries, except for those involving national security concerns and cultural considerations such as the mass media. Certain sectors subject to international negotiations over foreign investment such as the communications and shipping industries will also remain controlled.

Foreigners will be treated equally with Korean nationals when purchasing land for business purposes as well as non-business purposes. All limits on foreign investment in the local bond and money market have already been eliminated, as has the ceiling on foreign investment in the stock market. Foreign banks and securities companies are also allowed to establish local subsidiaries.

As of May 25, 1998, foreign investors have been able to buy shares of any Korean firm without consent of the board of directors or governmental approval, except for defense industry companies and public corporations. Foreigners can now purchase up to 50 percent of the outstanding shares of some public corporation.

All types of takeovers, including hostile acquisitions of Korean corporations, are permitted by both

Korean government officials discuss promotion of foreign investment in an international seminar.

domestic and foreign investors. Furthermore, foreign exchange transactions will be authorized for all financial institutions meeting certain requirements.

In May 1998, the aggregate ceiling on foreign investment in Korean equities was abolished.

Government bonds to be issued over the next two or three years will carry a maturity of three years. These bonds will be issued on a monthly basis.

Korea has also developed an institutional framework for mutual funds so that these funds can function as a key instrument for long-term financing. Private investors, both domestic and foreign, are now allowed to easily establish mutual funds in Korea. No qualification requirements are being imposed on investors who are sponsoring new mutual funds, with only minor standard exceptions. In essence, equal treatment has been guaranteed.

Investor-Oriented Support System

All current laws and regulations related to FDI have been streamlined and incorporated into a single legal framework represented by the new Foreign Investment Promotion Act (FIPA), which took effect in November 1998. This will enable foreign investors to take advantage of one-stop service and uniform national treatment.

Various incentive measures, including tax exemptions and reductions, have been instituted to promote FDI. To cite an example, corporate and income taxes will be exempted or reduced for businesses in targeted industries, such as the high-tech sector, for a period of 10 years. Government-owned real property will be leased to foreign-invested firms for up to 50 years at favorable rates, and for no cost in certain instances. Also, a free-trade investment zone will be developed to accommodate large-scale FDI. The government continued to phase out import restrictions, reducing the number of items subject to tariffs.

Service Sector

Liberalization of Korea's service sector has been difficult due to the relatively underdeveloped state of domestic service industries. Nevertheless, the government has taken a number of unilateral actions toward its eventual full opening. To cite some examples, the life insurance industry is now completely open to foreign underwriters.

Foreign banks receive treatment commensurate to that of national banks. Investment by foreigners in retailing and wholesaling activities is also open, although certain restrictions exist in specific areas. The advertising market, once open only to joint ventures with minority foreign participation, is now completely accessible to foreigners.

Intellectual Property Rights

The government recognizes that the strict protection of intellectual property rights is essential for the technological well-being of the nation and for cooperative economic relations with major trading partners. Consequently, since 1987 the government has instituted fundamental reforms to strengthen the protection of intellectual property rights.

New copyright law ensures comprehensive protection for both foreign and domestic works. Copyright guarantees extend over the life of an author plus 50 years. Also, safeguards against intellectual property infringement have been extended to computer software products through specific legislation.

Agricultural Market

In Korea, as in many countries, agricultural policy is fraught with far-reaching social and political implications, making liberalization of this sector a daunting challenge.

Korean sensitivity about agriculture derives in part from the fact that arable land per farmer in Korea is only 1/223 that of the United States, which makes it impossible for Korean farmers to be as competitive as their U.S. counterparts. Nonetheless, the Korean government is making efforts to further open the domestic agricultural market. These efforts are accompanied by continuing government initiatives to strengthen the competitiveness of Korea's agricultural sector.

In December 1988, the government formed a task force to revise the schedules for agricultural import liberalization through 1991. Revised plans have helped to increase the scope of liberalization and accelerate the pace of market opening. Also, during the Uruguay Round of the GATT (General

Agreement on Tariffs & Trade) negotiations on agricultural products, Korea committed to improving market access for various agricultural products.

Outlook for the Economy

Korea has been rapidly integrating itself into the world economy since the onset of the 1997 crisis. The government has advanced a new paradigm that involves upgrading business practices to international standards, promoting human resources and technology development and enhancing institutional efficiency.

The timing and strength of the economic recovery will depend largely on the pace of corporate sector restructuring, household adjustment to reduced job security and investor confidence in Korea. The government remains strongly committed to reform and will continue to implement financial and corporate restructuring while pursuing flexible macroeconomic policies conducive to growth.

Korea's goal is to solve the problems rooted in its past and create an economic structure suitable for an advanced economy meeting the challenges of the 21st century.

Social Welfare

Employment

The employment structure of Korea has undergone a noticeable transformation since the dawn of industrialization in the early 1960s. In 1960, workers engaged in the agricultural, forestry and fishery sectors accounted for 63 percent of the total labor force. However, this figure dropped to a mere 9.7 percent by 2002. By contrast, the weight of the tertiary indus-

Composition of Labor Force by Industry

(unit: percentage)

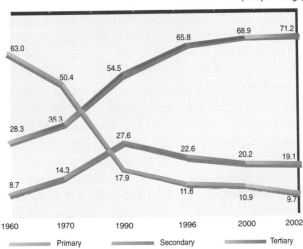

	1960	1970	1990	1996	2000	2002
Primary	63.0	50.4				
		35.3	27.6	22.6	20.2	19.1
Secondary	28.3	14.3	17.9			
			54.5	65.8	68.9	71.2
Tertiary	8.7		11.6		10.9	9.7

<Source: Ministry of Finance and Economy>

Note: The term "Primary" refers to the agricultural, forestry, hunting and fishery sectors; "Secondary," the mining and manufacturing sectors; and "Tertiary," social overhead capital (SOC) and the service sectors.

try (service sectors) has gone up from 28.3 percent of the total labor force in 1960 to 71.2 percent in 2002.

In the latter half of the 1970s, the Korean labor market went through a series of major changes. Korea emerged as a competitive country in the global market with its labor-intensive industry such as textiles and footwear. And the stabilization of supply and demand in the Korean labor market enabled workers to demand their rights, which resulted in the organization of an increasing number of trade unions and collective action. The wages of Korean workers has sharply increased since then.

As Korea faced the economic crisis of 1997-98, a national consensus has been established on the need for a flexible labor market. In March 1998, the government introduced a law which permits companies to lay off employees if there is no other feasible alternative. The law has been in effect since June 1998.

The measures taken to minimize job losses include various subsidies provided to small and medium enterprises to help them stabilize their management and retain their employees. The government has already been providing jobs to the unemployed through the early implementation of public investment projects and the expansion of public works projects since the beginning of the economic crisis. To ensure the creation of more jobs, it is also improving employment opportunities by promoting the start-up of export and venture firms and including foreign investment by allowing hostile acquisition of Korean companies by foreign investors. For this purpose, the relevant laws have been revised to simplify the procedures in Korea.

To develop and enhance the job skills of the unemployed, the government has expanded vocational

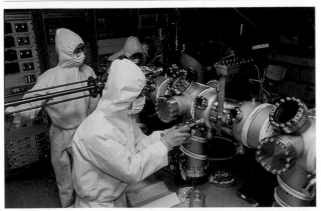

Employees in the precision engineering industry

training programs. In addition, a one-stop service system has been set up to integrate unemployment benefits, vocational training and employment security institutions.

The operation of overseas job placement agencies have been authorized once again. A center for overseas unemployment has been opened, and a plan to provide more opportunities for overseas employment, such as overseas job fairs, has been established.

The government is also working closely with the Korea International Cooperation Agency (KOICA) to find overseas voluntary service opportunities for the unemployed.

The livelihood protection support from the government has been extended to low-income people who remain unemployed for a long period of time, covering living expenses, school fees for children and medical care.

The Employment Insurance System (EIS), which was established in 1995, initially covered only full-time employees at workplaces with 30 workers or more. It was extended to cover those at workplaces with five workers or more in March 1998, and further extended to cover all workers including part-time and temporary workers as of October 1999.

The Tripartite Committee, launched in 1998, comprising representatives from labor, business and the government has worked to create social consensus so that all three concerned parties share the pain and efforts in overcoming the economic crisis.

Housing

As in other countries, industrialization in Korea proceeded in line with its urbanization. In 1960, only 38.0 percent of Korea's population lived in cities. By 2000, 88.3 percent of Korea's population lived in cities.

This rapid population growth in urban areas led to a housing shortage and spiraling land prices in cities. In order to solve the housing shortage problem and stabilize housing costs, increasing the supply of land available for residential construction and the building of small housing units have continuously been one of the top priorities of the government.

In 1988, the government established and promoted its "Two Million Housing Units Construction Plan" for the period of 1988-1992. Actual housing construction for the period totaled 2.7 million units, and this massive supply contributed to a sharp stabilization of previously rising housing prices.

The government has supplied an average of 500,000 to 600,000 housing units per year from 1993 to 1997. As a result of these efforts, the housing supply ratio increased to 100.6 percent in 2002 from 72.4 percent in 1990.

In Korea, housing rental involves a unique system.

Apartment complex on Yeouido Island

Rentals with monthly payments are rare, with most rentals requiring the payment of a lump sum deposit, usually ranging between 50 to 70 percent of the housing unit price. The deposit is refunded when the contract expires. This system, known as *jeonse*, gives the property owner profit in the form of interest on the deposit. About 66 percent of those who resided in rental housing in 2002 rented the unit using this system.

With rising land prices and modernization of lifestyles due to economic growth, the ratio of people living in apartment buildings has continued to increase as well. As recently as 1985, only 13.5 percent of households lived in apartments, but by 2002, 47.7 percent of households lived in apartments. The ratio is higher in larger cities with nearly half of all households (55 percent) in the nation's seven metropolitan cities living in apartments.

Health and Medical Services

Due to Korea's success in economic development, the overall health of Koreans has improved significantly over the past three decades. In 1960, the life expectancy at birth was 51 years for males and 54 for females. These figures have increased to 72.1 for males and 79.5 for females in 2000. The infant mortality rate has likewise declined sharply, along with maternal mortality as well.

These improvements are all directly related to improvement in diet as well as in available health and medical services. The Ministry of Health and Welfare (MOHW) is responsible for all aspects of health services, including the strategic planning for the maintenance and promotion of national health and social welfare. The annual budget of MOHW has been growing in recent years. In 2003, it amounted to 8.35 trillion won (approximately US$6.7 billion).

People are relying on medicine and medical services with growing frequency, and the share of medical costs to total household expenditures has increased accordingly. In 1985, national health expenditure per capita was 85,000 won which increased to 654,000 won in 2000.

Health care in the form of medical insurance and medical assistance was first introduced in 1977. However, the coverage rate was only 29.5 percent up until 1980. As of 2002, 96.97 percent of the population had access to health insurance, with the remaining 3.03 percent being able to receive direct medical assistance.

The supply of hospitals and medical personnel has continuously increased. The total number of hospitals and clinics in the nation (including Oriental medicine hospitals and clinics) was 11,188 in 1975, which increased to 40,276 in 2001. Meanwhile, the number of licensed doctors, that totaled 16,800 in 1975, increased to 75,295 in 2001.

National statistics for 2000 showed that there was one physician for every 556 persons, one dentist for every 2,609 and one pharmacist for every 929.

Social Security

Various systems related to social security have been implemented since the late 1980s. These included expansion of medical insurance and medical assistance in 1988 and 1989, and the introduction of an Unemployment Insurance System in 1995. The government has thus provided the basis for building a society that can ensure the well-being of its people.

The National Pension System, when first introduced in 1988, covered employees at workplaces with 10 or more workers. It was revised to cover workers in workplaces with five or more employees in 1992 and was expanded to cover those engaged in agriculture and the self-employed in rural areas in 1995. Finally, it came to cover the entire nation in 1999.

While the primary goal of the above systems is to provide minimum guarantees to the economically active population in the case of economic difficulties, there are also welfare programs directed to those not economically active. These public subsidy programs consist mainly of the following two parts: subsidies for living expenses and medical assistance.

Due to increased living standards and the improvement in health and medical services, the average age of Koreans has increased rapidly, which means that the number of elderly has increased significantly over the years. In 1960, the population aged 65 and over comprised 2.9 percent of Korea's total population. By 2002, this ratio had increased to 7.9 percent, and is expected to rise to 14.4 percent by 2019.

Obstetricians providing quality medical care.

Policies that have been implemented to improve the welfare of the elderly include the following: the provision of direct subsidies to the elderly living under the subsistence level, the expanding of employment opportunities for older people by developing suitable jobs and opening job placement centers, the strengthening of health care systems for the aged, and the opening of various types of public facilities for the elderly.

With the strengthening of social security measures since the late 1980s, awareness of the needs of the handicapped has been increasing. In February 2003, the Ministry of Health and Welfare developed a "The Second Five-Year Welfare Development Plan for the Handicapped 2000-2005," which is to be implemented in cooperation with other executive branches of the government, including the Ministry of Education and Human Resources Development and the Ministry of Labor etc.

This development plan envisages, first, to improve overall welfare by expanding public subsidy programs, installing more facilities for the handicapped in public places, and building more welfare centers; second, to increase the number of educational institutions that provide job training; and third, to increase employment opportunities by providing subsidies to employers for installing necessary facilities.

Women

In traditional Korean society, women's roles were confined to the home. From a young age, women were taught the virtues of subordination and endurance to prepare for their future roles as wife and mother. Women, in general, could not participate in society as men did, and their role was limited to household matters.

The situation began to change with the opening of the country to the outside world during the late 19th century. During this period, modern schools were introduced, mostly by Western Christian missionaries. Some of these schools were founded with the specific goal of educating women. These educated women began to engage in the arts, teaching, religious work, and enlightening other women. Women also took part in the independence movement against the Japanese occupation, and displayed no less vigor, determination, and courage than the men.

With the establishment of the Republic of Korea in 1948, women achieved constitutional rights for equal opportunities to pursue education, work, and public life. There is no doubt that the female labor force contributed significantly to the rapid economic growth that Korea achieved during the past three decades.

As economic development proceeded and the living conditions of Koreans improved, the educational attainment level of women also increased. In 1966, among those graduating from elementary school, only 33 percent of girls continued their education in middle school. The comparable figures for high school and university were 20 percent and 4 percent, respectively, during the same period. However, by 1998, the comparable ratios reached 99.5 percent and 61.6 percent for high school and university. The economic participation rate of women also has increased steadily since industrialization from 34.4 percent in 1965 to 48.1 percent in 1999.

In terms of characteristics of the female labor force, in 1975, only 2 percent of the female labor force worked in professional or managerial occupations, while 4 percent worked in clerical positions. However, by 1998, 12.6 percent of female employees were serving in professional or managerial positions, and another 16 percent were working in clerical occupations.

With an increasing number of women entering professional jobs, the government passed the "Equal Employment Act" in 1987 to prevent discriminatory practices against female workers in regard to hiring and promotion opportunities.

Korean women today are actively engaged in a wide variety of fields, including education, medicine, engineering, scholarship, the arts, law, literature, and sports. Women are thus making significant contributions to society.

With the launch of the new Administration in 1998, the Presidential Commission on Women's Affairs was established to handle issues specifically involving women. The commission was elevated and expanded to become the Ministry of Gender Equality in January 2001. The new ministry set up 20 specific tasks to be achieved in six basic areas. These areas

An increasing number of women work in professional fields.

are: to revise and establish laws and rules that involve discrimination in any sector and to increase the representation of women, to facilitate women's employment and provide support for female workers, to increase educational opportunities for women to be competitive in the labor market, to provide social welfare policies for women, to promote women's involvement in various social activities including volunteer work and women's organization activities, and to strengthen the cooperation of Korean women's organizations with international women's organizations.

Education

Overview

Koreans have traditionally placed great importance on education as a means for self-fulfillment as well as for social advancement. Modern schools were introduced in the 1880s. With the founding of the Republic of Korea in 1948, the government began to establish a modern educational system, making the six years of elementary school attendance mandatory in 1953. Today, Korea boasts one of the highest literacy rates in the world, and it is a well recognized fact that Korea's well-educated people have been the primary source of the rapid economic growth that the nation has achieved during the past three decades.

The Ministry of Education and Human Resources Development is the government body responsible for the formulation and implementation of educational policies. The government provides guidance on basic policy matters as well as financial assistance. The financing of education is centralized, and government funding constitutes the largest component of school budgets.

The School System

Although preschool education is not yet compulsory, its importance has been increasingly recognized in recent years. As recently as 1980, there were only 901 kindergartens across the nation but this number

Education System

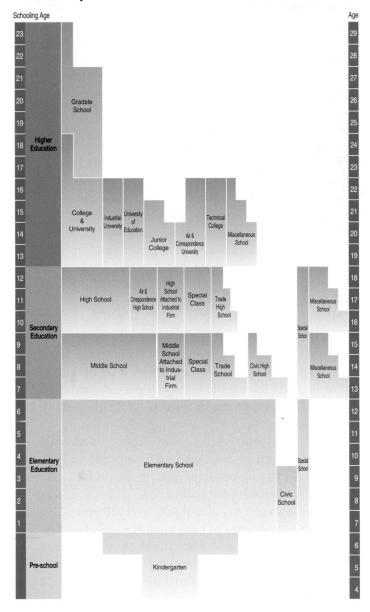

Schooling Age | Age

- Higher Education
  - Gradate School
  - College & University
  - Industrial University
  - University of Education
  - Junior College
  - Air & Correspondence University
  - Technical College
  - Miscellaneous School
- Secondary Education
  - High School
  - Air & Crrespondence High School
  - High School Attached to Industrial Firm
  - Special Class
  - Trade High School
  - Middle School
  - Middle School Attached to Industrial Firm
  - Special Class
  - Trade School
  - Civic High School
  - Miscellaneous School
  - Special School
- Elementary Education
  - Elementary School
  - Civic School
  - Special School
- Pre-school
  - Kindergarten

has increased to 8,343 as of 2002. The government has carried out a nationwide project to subsidize kindergarten tuition for children from low-income families since September 1999, providing underprivileged children increased opportunities for preschool education and thereby establishing a more equitable educational environment. The program was expanded to provide free education for 20 percent of five-year-old children from 2002.

The education system in the Republic of Korea consists of six-year elementary schools, three-year middle schools, three-year high schools, and four-year colleges and universities, which also offer graduate courses leading to Ph.D. degrees. There are also two- to three-year junior colleges and vocational colleges as well. Elementary schooling is compulsory with an enrollment rate of 100 percent. Three more years of compulsory education for the middle school course was implemented nationwide in 2002.

The average number of students per teacher in elementary schools stood at 58.8 in 1960. This figure has been reduced to 28.1 in 2002. The average number of students in a class was 34.9 in 2002. It will be reduced to 31.2 by 2003. Four-year educational study at a teacher's university is required of an elementary school teacher.

Upon completion of elementary school, children in the twelve to fourteen age group enter the middle school system for seventh to ninth grade courses. The student-teacher ratio for middle schools in 2002 was 19.3, while the comparable figure for 1970 was 42.3.

There are two types of high schools in the Republic of Korea, general and vocational. Applicants for vocational high schools (covering agriculture, engineering, business and maritime studies) have a

Elementary school pupils enjoying outdoor activities.

choice of schools and are admitted through examinations administered by each school. The curriculum at vocational high schools is usually 40-60 percent general courses with the remainder being vocational courses. As of 2002, there were 741 vocational high schools with 535,363 students. Among general high schools, there are several specialized high schools in the areas of arts, physical education, science, and foreign languages. The goal of these schools is to provide appropriate education for students with special ability in certain fields.

Courses at general high schools tend to center around preparations for entering universities. As of 2002, there were 1,254 general high schools with 1.22 million students. Combining the two types of high school together, the ratio of middle school graduates advancing to high school was 99.5 in 2002.

The curriculum, revised in 1997, introduces ten basic common subjects, individual projects and special activities that cover the ten years from the first year of elementary school through to the first year of high school. It also includes new elective subjects for

Computer education programs for middle school students

the final two years of high school that are designed to provide students greater direction in discovering their aptitudes and more choices in choosing their future careers.

The new curricula were put into effect, beginning with kindergartens, in 2000. The introduction of the curricula in elementary schools started with the first and second grades in 2000, followed by the 3rd and 4th grades in 2001 and by the 5th and 6th grades in 2002. In middle schools and high schools, it was applied to first year students and freshmen in 2001 and 2002 respectively.

There are several different types of institutions of higher learning in the Republic of Korea: colleges and universities with four-year undergraduate programs (six years for medical and dental colleges), four-year teacher's universities, two-year junior vocational colleges, an air and correspondence university, open universities, and miscellaneous schools of collegiate status with two- or four-year programs such as nursing schools and theological seminaries. As of 2002, there were 358 institutions of higher learning in Korea, with a total of 3.31 million students and 59,750 faculty members.

Colleges and universities in Korea operate under strict enrollment limits. The eligibility of each applicant is determined by the student's high school records and national standardized test results. In addition to this, certain colleges and universities require an additional entrance essay test administered by each institution since 1996.

In 2002, the ratio of high school graduates who advanced to institutions of higher learning was 87 percent for general high schools and 49.8 percent for vocational high schools.

Special Education and Non-formal Education

With an increasing awareness of the needs of the handicapped, the number of special schools for the handicapped has steadily increased in recent years. As of 2002, there were 136 schools for the handicapped in the nation with a total of 23,453 students.

These include 12 for students with visual impairments, 20 for students with hearing impairments, 18 for students with physical disabilities, and 86 for students with mental retardation.

In addition to these special schools, some general schools also have been providing integrated schooling for handicapped students by opening special classes within their schools. To improve the quality of special education, the government established the National Special Education Institute in 1994, which has been responsible for developing special education programs and providing training for teachers.

Korea National Open University provides working youth and adults with four-year post-high school courses in business administration, agriculture, education, public administration, and home economics. The University broadcasts 14 30-minute programs on radio and one 30-minute EBS-TV program as well as 18 hours of broadcasts per day on the Open University Network, a cable-TV channel and satellite broadcasting.

Those who complete the required credit units receive the same type of degree as the graduates of regular colleges and universities. There are also distance-learning and correspondence high school programs. Other types of non-traditional education programs include various training courses offered by government agencies and private organizations. Subjects taught in these classes range from special vocational skills to techniques in the arts, with the goal of assisting youth and adults in their job performance or leisure activities.

Korean Studies

The term Korean studies emerged after national liberation in 1945, with the academic community's efforts to enhance research on Korea, including its history, culture, and socio-political system. Academic research had been suppressed or dominated by a Japanese point of view during the 35-year-long colonial period. While an increasing number of foreign scholars were engaged in Korean studies in recent decades, the government supported domestic research activities through the Academy of Korean Studies established in 1978 and the Korean Studies Graduate School which opened two years later. As of 2002, the state-run academy has produced 427 masters and 140 doctorate degree holders in six majors - philosophy and religion, history, language and litera-

University students on campus

ture and classical studies, arts, society and folklore, politics and economy, and education and ethics. The academy now has 171 students enrolled in its masters and Ph.D.-integrated programs. Foreign graduates have returned to their home countries where they are active as professors or researchers of Korean studies.

Korean studies have attracted mounting attention from intellectuals overseas with related courses now available at some 338 universities in China, Japan, Thailand, Denmark, the United States, Russia, Switzerland, Germany, Poland, Ukraine, Hungary and other countries. Foreigners may also enroll in Korean language courses at universities in Seoul, including Seoul National University, Yonsei University, Korea University and Ewha Womans University.

Transportation and Communications

Transportation

Subway System

Seoul's subway system is the largest in the country and transports about 5.5 million passengers a day. It first went into service in 1974 with the opening of Line 1 and now consists of 8 lines extending nearly 287 kilometers with stops at 263 stations providing links between almost all destination points in the metropolitan Seoul area.

Subway service is also available in 3 other cities: Busan, Daegu, and Incheon. Two lines in operation in Busan, which first began subway service in 1985,

Line 5 of the Seoul subway system has a stop at Gimpo Airport.

span 70.5 kilometers in length with 73 stops in major downtown and suburban locations and carries over 711,000 people a day. Daegu's Line 1, opened in 1997, runs 25.9 kilometers through 30 stations. Incheon commenced subway service in October 1999 and now links 22 stations travelling through 21.9 kilometers. Still under construction are Phase 3 of Line 2 and Line 3 in Busan, Line 2 in Daegu, Lines 2 and 3 in Incheon, and new subways in Daejeon and Gwangju.

Subways systems in Korea feature the most up-to-date facilities and are fast becoming the most preferred mode of mass transportation for its convenience.

Railway

As of 2002, the railway system of Korea encompassed 64 routes spanning 3,129 operational kilometers. The railway plays an important role in inter-city passenger and freight transport. The Korean National Railroad (KNR) possesses 2,850 locomotives and 18,559 rail cars in all of which 1,596 are passenger cars and 14,113 are freight cars. The express train, Saemaeul, travels the distance of 444 kilometers between Seoul and Busan in about 4 hours.

For railway traffic safety and efficiency, KNR operates the Centralized Traffic Control System (CTC), which regulates Seoul suburban lines and the Gyeongbu, Jungang, Taebaek, and Yeongdong lines covering 1,321 kilometers. All these lines are equipped with an automatic train stop system to help prevent accidents.

Gyeongbu High-Speed Rail is under construction at present. With its start in 1992, Phase 1 of the project consists of new high-speed rail construction from Seoul to Daegu and will upgrade the existing line from Daegu to Busan. It is scheduled to be completed in April 2004 and will cut travel time from Seoul to Busan to 2 hours and 40 minutes. Phase 2 will see the completion of a new high-speed line from Daegu to Busan in 2010, where the travel time will be less than 2 hours. It is expected to ease current traffic congestion on highways and offer greater convenience to the public.

Automobiles

Motor vehicle registration in Korea increased dramatically from 527,729 in 1980 to 13,949,440 in 2002 due to steady rise in income and living standards, expansion of suburbs, and development of the car manufacturing industry. This is an average annual increase of about 19 percent. In particular, passenger cars saw the largest increase jumping from 249,102 to 9,737,428, more than 38 times. The number of other vehicles registered as of 2002 are 1,275,319 passenger/cargo combined cars, 2,894,412 trucks, and 42,281 special vehicles.

Buses and Taxis

Mainly there are 3 types of buses–urban, airport limousine, and express in Korea servicing routes throughout metropolitan areas and beyond. In Seoul, for example, Urban (or intra-city) buses run on major corridors of the city, airport limousine buses run to and from the Incheon International Airport and urban centers and other suburbs in the metropolitan area, and express buses operate between all principal cities in the country providing linkages outside of Seoul.

Taxis play a vital role in meeting transportation needs in large cities and are divided into 2 types; regular and deluxe taxis. Deluxe taxis charge higher fares and aim to provide better services. All deluxe

Intercity highways make possible one-day trips to destinations.

taxis and many regular taxis offer free interpretation service in English, Japanese and Chinese through mobile phone connection for the convenience of foreign visitors with language barriers.

As in many other industrializing nations, cities in Korea face problems such as traffic congestion and limited parking spaces. In order to alleviate these problems, the government introduced measures such as bus-only lanes and transport cards to improve bus transportation service so as to encourage more commuters to leave their cars at home.

Various Transportation Demand Management (TDM) measures have also been implemented to effectively manage passenger car traffic. Such measures include congestion toll at Namsan Tunnels, discount on Traffic Impact Fees for employers adopting programs, e.g. car-pooling, to help reduce traffic volume, and flexible pricing for parking which allows higher parking fees in congested areas.

Expressways

Expressways connect Seoul with provincial cities and towns placing any destination in Korea within a day's travel. The 24-kilometer Seoul-Incheon Expressway, completed in 1968, was the first modern highway built in Korea. The much longer 425.5-kilometer Seoul-Busan Expressway was completed two years later marking a great stride forward in the nation's efforts to expand and modernize its transportation network. Today, there are 23 expressways covering all parts of the country and measuring 2,637 kilometers in all.

International and Domestic Air Transport

Korea has air service agreements with 81 countries and major international airlines now offer over 1,400 scheduled direct or non-stop flights per week from Korea to major cities in North America, Europe, the Middle East, and Asia.

In 1969, when the government owned and run Korean Air Lines (KAL) was privatized, KAL had only two jet aircraft. Today, the entire fleet of KAL and Asiana Airlines exceeds 180 passenger and cargo aircraft and the number continues to grow.

Internationally, KAL and Asiana Airlines serve 87 cities around the world ranking 4th in the world in annual cargo handling capacity and 11th in passenger transport. Domestically, the two airlines serve 15 cities: Seoul, Busan, Jeju, Daegu, Gwangju, Jinju, Wonju, Cheongju, Yeosu, Ulsan, Mokpo, Gunsan, Yangyang, Yecheon, and Pohang. The two carriers transported more than 20 million people to these destinations in 2001.

Incheon International Airport, opened in March 2001, is equipped with state-of-the-art facilities and provides advanced traffic networks for its customers. The new airport, optimally located geographically, is being fostered to become the leading hub airport in Northeast Asia to further boost Korea's growth into a

The Incheon International Airport

major center of logistics. Plans for the airport include a Free Trade Zone, International Business District, and Special Economic Zone.

Maritime Transportation

Container ships from Korea ply the international sea lanes to ports in South and North America, Europe, Australia, the Middle East and Africa. Foreign ocean liners, cruise ships and passenger-carrying freighters also pay frequent visits to Korean ports. The annual cargo handling capability of Korea's ports in 2000 amounted to about 430 million tons, which is some 47.7 times greater than the 9 million tons in 1961. In 1996, the government upgraded the Korea Maritime and Port Administration, established in 1976, into the Ministry of Maritime Affairs and Fisheries. This change reflects the increasing importance of maritime transportation in national development. It is now the major government body responsible for promoting development of the maritime transportation industry.

Communications

Postal Service

The Directorate General of Posts was inaugurated in 1884 with the mandate to introduce modern postal services in Korea. As of 2002, there were 3,709 post offices operating throughout the country, with each myeon (a group of several villages) being served by one or more post offices. In 2002, the mail volume totaled 4,498 million items. Most letters were delivered within three working days, except in some remote areas.

The speed and efficiency of the mail delivery process has greatly improved since the introduction of the first computerized mail centers in 1990. As of 2002, twenty two mail centers were equipped with the latest automated letter and parcel sorting machines. Plans are under way to build another 3 mail centers nationwide by 2006.

A total of 3,709 post offices provide not only postal services but also various banking services such as deposit, remittance and life insurance services. To meet the increasing needs of customers, Korea Post has been introducing various new services including Flower Delivery Service, e-Post, Mail Order Services, Computer Mail Services, etc.

In 1998, Korea Post was able to overcome its chronic deficit status and recorded a surplus for the first time in its history. Its outstanding performance continued throughout 2002, achieving its fifth consecutive years of surplus.

To meet the fast changing business environment, Korea Post was reorganized as an independent governmental agency under the auspices of the Ministry of Information and Communication in July 2000.

The number of cellular phones and PCS users has been increasing.

The new organization, the Office of Postal Service has attained a greater degree of autonomy and is now responsible for its own structure, budget, and operations.

Telephone and Mobile Communication Services

A 30-kilometer telegraph line from Seoul to the west coast city of Incheon, completed in September 1885, marked the first modern communications service in Korea. This service gradually replaced signal fires, which had been the major means of communication over extended distances.

The first telephones in Korea were installed in the royal palace compound in 1896, public telephone service was introduced in 1902, and international telephone service began in 1924 between Seoul and Fengtian, China.

An adequate infrastructure for modern communications, however, was not envisioned until 1962 under the Five-Year Telecommunications Plan. Up until the 1980s, though, the importance of communications to a modern society was not fully appreciated. As of the

end of 1979, there were only some 240,000 telephone subscribers, about 6.3 telephones per 100 people.

In 1982, the government set up Korea Telecom to
take over the telephone and telegraph business from
the Ministry of Communications. A result of active
R&D investment, in 1986, enabled Korea to become
the 10th nation in the world to develop an electronic
switching system, known as TDX-1. With this technology, Korea has provided an additional one million
circuits annually.

The number of telephone lines in Korea exceeded
10 million in 1987, with virtually every household
having a telephone. International Subscriber Dialing
(ISD) services also have been available since then.
As of the end of 2000, the number of telephone lines
reached 29 million with subscribers totaling 22 million. The number of telephones per 100 persons has
increased to 58, and all telephone circuits are now
connected by automatic switching systems.

After Mobile communications service began in
Korea in 1984 and the number of cellular phone
users gradually increased in the 1980s. Since 1990
the speed of increasement on the users has become
much faster and the total subscribers stood at 32mil-
lion as of the end of 2002. Along with the increasement of subscriber numbers, the mobile communication service that had simply offered voice or message
transmission services evolved to provide data, wire-
less internet and video streaming services in earnest.

Korea launched CDMA2000-1x commercial services that enabled multimedia service for the first
time in the world in April 2001, and started
CDMA2000-1x EV DO service that makes available
full-fledged 3G mobile communication services

Website of the Korean Overseas Information Service
(http://www.korea.net)

including video streaming in May 2002.

As of the end of December 2002, mobile subscribers for CDMA2000-1x amounted to 17million, accounting for 51.1% of the total cellular phone users, and the number of its subscribers is expected to steadily grow.

As for 2GHz IMT-2000 service, three local operators were granted with a license, and they greatly contributed to earning the nation greater recognition as IT Korea by showcasing and providing trial services during the opening ceremony and football matches of the 2002 Korea/Japan FIFA World Cup. 2GHz IMT-2000 service based on W-CDMA technology will be deployed in the second half of 2003.

Computer-Related Communications

With the rapid development of the IT industry and the explosive proliferation of computers, more and more Koreans are using computer-related communications – on-line services and the Internet.

The number of on-line service subscribers increased from 718,000 in 1995 to 17 million in 2001, while the number of Internet users soared from

366,000 to 24.3 million during the same period.

In recognition of the ever-increasing need for building a networked society to prepare for the coming information age, the government launched its plan to build an information super-highway in 1995.

The first stage of the plan was completed in 1997, and the second stage was completed at the end of 2000. A high-speed and high-quality optical transmission network of 155 Mbps-40 Gbps has been established in 144 cities. A commercial ATM network was constructed by installing 361 ATM switches and connecting the access equipment of 198 subscribers to major cities across the nation.

With the successful implementation of the plan, Korea now possesses a high-speed network infrastructure that offers high-quality data services nationwide, positioning the nation as one of the world's 10 most advanced countries in terms of information networks.

Broadband internet service was first introduced in Korea in July 1998 when Korea Thrunet rolled out the service using cable modem. Afterwards, broadband internet has shown drastic growth backed by new broadband services such as ADSL, VDSL and the government's promotion policy as it can be seen broadband subscribers exceeding 10 million. Based on such an astounding achievement, the ITU and OECD recognized Korea as number one country worldwide in terms of broadband penetration and utilization.

Down the road, broadband Internet appears to see continuous growth in the number of users thanks to a wide arrange of services to be offered through the expansion of broadband networks. And ultimately this will lead to enhance quality of life of people.

The Media

Newspaper and News Agencies

As of December 2001, there were a total of 121 daily newspapers across the country. Of those, 86 are general newspapers – 22 nationwide papers and 64 local dailies – and 29 are industry newspapers specializing in business, education or sports. Six newspapers are published in foreign languages, five in English and one in Chinese.

The Korean press is now well over a century old. Korea's first modern newspaper, the *Dongnip Sinmun* (Independence Newspaper), was established in 1896 by Dr. Seo Jae-pil. The *Dongnip Sinmum* was a bilingual paper with 300 copies of four tabloid pages printed three times a week, the first three pages in Korean and the last page in English.

Over the following decades, Korean newspapers found their greatest challenge in upholding the nationalistic spirit of the Korean people and opening their eyes to the rapidly changing world. The newspapers played an important role in independence movements during the Japanese colonial regime (1910-1945).

The *Chosun Ilbo* and the *Dong-A Ilbo* are the two oldest newspapers in Korea, both inaugurated in 1920 in the wake of the March First Independence Movement. Both newspapers are known for their independent editorial policies and considerable influence on public opinion. This spirit persisted through the establishment of the Republic of Korea in 1948. With broad leeway to criticize officialdom, newspapers have always been at the forefront of leading social changes.

Newspaper circulation has been increasing steadily, and the National Statistical Office indicates that circulation currently stands at 394 copies for every 1,000 persons. Korean newspapers have made significant investments in modern press facilities and equipment in recent years. Most national dailies operate computerized typesetting and editing systems with multicolor printing capability.

There are two major news agencies in Korea, Yonhap News and Newsis. With an extensive news-gathering network in the capital city and provinces, Yonhap News also maintains 19 overseas bureaus in Europe, North America, the Middle East, Southeast Asia, and South America. And Newsis which was registered in 2001 is now preparing to provide news services.

Television

Television broadcasting in the Republic of Korea began in 1956 with the opening of a privately-owned and commercially operated station in Seoul. This first TV station, however, was destroyed by fire in 1959. In December 1961, KBS-TV was inaugurated by the government as the first full-scale television service in Korea. Another broadcast firm, TBC-TV, began operation in December 1964. The Munhwa Broadcasting Corporation established Korea's third television station, MBC-TV, in August 1969. During a period of media mergers in the late 1980s, TBC-TV was taken over by KBS and renamed as KBS-2.

EBS (the Educational Broadcasting System), under

the supervision of the Ministry of Education, started broadcasting in 1990. EBS broadcasts extracurricular educational programs for students and also cultural programs and documentaries. EBS became a public corporation under the new Broadcasting Law in June 2000.

SBS (the Seoul Broadcasting System) began broadcasting under private management in 1990. The first privately-operated local stations –PSB (Busan Broadcasting Corp.), TBC (Daegu Broadcasting Corp.), KBC (Gwangju Broadcasting Company) and TJB (Daejeon Broadcasting Corp.)– were established in 1995 to promote local culture and develop local economy. A second group of privately-operated local stations –iTV (Incheon Television Corp.), UBC (Ulsan Broadcasting Corp.), CJB (Cheongju Broadcasting Corp.) and JTV (Jeonju Television Corp.)– began operating in 1997.

Additionally, Gangwon Television Broadcasting (GTB) and Jeju Free International City Broadcasting System (JIBS) started broadcasting services in 2001 and 2002 respectively.

The KBS, MBC, SBS and EBS television networks launched digital broadcasting in the Seoul metropolitan area from the latter half of 2001. The services will be expanded to the greater Seoul and surrounding areas in 2002.

Cable TV was first introduced in Korea in 1970. It was popular especially among those who could not enjoy good TV reception due to geographical conditions or man-made structures.

However, since the late 1980s, as public demand for more information and a greater variety of entertainment increased, demand for cable TV has also been on the increase.

Catalyst for changes in lifestyle, Digital Broadcasting, which is in the form of HDTV (high-definition TV).

Cable TV started experimental services in 1991. As of the end of 2001, 8 million subscribers were able to view about 60 cable channels broadcasting programs in 77 subject areas.

Korea has put three telecommunications satellites - Mugunghwa Nos. 1, 2, 3 into orbit since 1995 and secured 168 satellite channels to broadcast programs in such diverse areas as sports, music, education and entertainment. The Korea Digital Broadcasting (KDB) launched a satellite broadcasting service in March 2002 and as of the end of 2002, it was providing diverse channel services to about 500,000 subscribers. The satellites also paved the way for Korea to become one of the leading nations in information technology.

Radio

Radio broadcasting in Korea started in 1927, when the Japanese government established a station in

Seoul. The U.S. military government in Korea subsequently took it over and later formed the Korea Broadcasting System (KBS). This was the only radio station in the country until 1954, when the Christian Broadcasting System (CBS), operated chiefly with contributions from churches, started educational and religious programming along with news and entertainment broadcasts.

In December 1956, another Christian organization, the Evangelical Alliance Mission, inaugurated the Far East Broadcasting Station in Incheon, and the first commercial radio enterprise in Korea, the Busan Munhwa Broadcasting Station, was established in Busan in April 1959. The founding of several private broadcasting companies followed. MBC (Munhwa Broadcasting Company) began operations in December 1961 with call sign KLKV, followed by two rivals, DBS (Dong-A Broadcasting Station) in 1963 and TBC (Dongyang Broadcasting Company) in 1964.

Another wave of change took place in 1990, with the establishment of a number of specialized broadcasting stations. The Seoul city-operated TBS (Traffic Broadcasting Station) was set up in June 1990, followed by the government-operated EBS (Educational Broadcasting Station). Peace Broadcasting Foundation for Catholics and the Buddhist Broadcasting System were also established in 1990.

In March 1991, the privately-owned Seoul Radio Station began broadcasting to a target audience among the Seoul Metropolitan area and its vicinity, while five other privately-owned local FM radio channels opened in 1997. There are presently a total of 254 radio stations in the Republic of Korea, comprising 136 FM stations and 59 AM stations. Despite the increasing popularity of television, radio still has an expanding audience in Korea.

Culture and the Arts

Korea, a peninsular nation, has developed several unique characteristics of its people due to its topographical peculiarities. The oceanic and continental inclinations combine to form the basis of the people's identity, which underlies the foundation of the country's culture and arts. Being a peninsula also involves a cultural environment with peripheral and centric features. Peripheral aspects relate to the continental cultures which flow into the peninsula, while its centric factors result from the peripheral cultures evolving and being restructured to form a new center.

Under this topographical influence, the Korean people came to develop a peace-loving yet dynamic character that has created a contemplative yet vibrant, optimistic yet sentimental culture.

UNESCO's World Heritage List

UNESCO has recognized the unique value and the distinct character of Korean culture, which is different from Chinese or Japanese culture, by placing a number of Korean treasures on its World Heritage List. The items and sites honored are the eighth century *Bulguksa* Temple and the *Seokguram* Grotto, both in Gyeongju, Gyeongsangbuk-do Province, the *Tripitaka Koreana* woodblocks (for printing Buddhist scriptures) and *Janggyeongpanjeon* (the ancient storage hall for these woodblocks) on the grounds of *Haeinsa* Temple in Gyeongsangnam-do Province, the *Jongmyo Shrine* and *Changdeokgung*

122

Listed on UNESCO's World Cultural Heritage List: Prehistoric dolmens, *Seokguram* Grotto, *Tripitaka Koreana* Woodblocks, *Jongmyo* Shrine, *the entire area of Gyeongju*, and *Changdeokgung* Palace, *Hwaseong* Fortress (Left to right and top to the bottom)

Palace in Seoul, and the *Hwaseong* Fortress in Suwon. In 2000, two more Korean treasures were added to the list: the prehistoric dolmens in Gochang, Hwasun and Ganghwa, and the entire area of Gyeongju, the capital of the ancient Silla Kingdom, where innumerable cultural treasures and historic sites are carefully preserved.

Bulguksa Temple was constructed over a 23-year period during the Silla Kingdom (57 B.C.-A.D. 935). Built on a series of stone terraces, *Bulguksa* appears to emerge organically from the rocky terrain of the wooded foothills of Mt. Tohamsan.

The temple features the *Seokgatap* and *Dabotap* pagodas, *Cheongungyo*, *Baegungyo* and *Chilbogyo* staircases that were called bridges because symbolically they lead from the secular world to *Bulguk*, the Land of the Buddha, a couple of gilted bronze Buddhas, and many other distinguished items within and outside the temple grounds.

Dominating the courtyard of *Daeungjeon* hall are two of Korea's most beautiful pagodas. The 8.3-meter-high *Seokgatap* (Pagoda of Sakyamuni) and the 10.5-meter-high *Dabotap* (Many Treasures Pagoda) were both built around 756. It is recorded that Kim Dae-seong built them for his parents, which is perhaps why the *Seokgatap* is rather masculine and the *Dabotap* feminine. *Seokgatap* is characterized by simplicity and princely dignity whereas *Dabotap* is highly decorative. The simple, three-story *Seokgatap* represents spiritual ascent via the rules put forth by Sakyamuni, whereas the more ornate *Dabotap* symbolizes the complexity of the world.

Seokguram Grotto was built simultaneously with *Bulguksa* Temple. It has undergone remodeling several times over the years. It is an artificially created stone cavern in which a total of 39 images of the Buddha can be found. The grotto, like the structures in the vicinity of *Bulguksa* Temple, is made from granite.

Seokguram comprises a rectangular antechamber and a round interior chamber with a domed ceiling connected by a passageway. Chiseled out of a single block of granite, the 3.5-meter-high main Buddha is seated cross-legged on a lotus throne facing the east, eyes closed in quiet meditation, a serene, all-knowing expression on its face.

Haeinsa Janggyeongpanjeon is the repository for the *Tripitaka Koreana*, consisting of more than 81,340 wooden printing blocks, the Goryeo version of the Buddhist canon. With more than 52 million Chinese character's precisely rendered, it is famous as the oldest and most comprehensive Buddhist canon existing in the world today.

Jongmyo Shrine was dedicated in 1395, three years after the Joseon Dynasty was established to preserve the remains of kings and queens. Ceremonial recreations of the ancestral worship rites of Joseon are conducted on the first Sunday of every May at *Jongmyo*. Special ceremonial music called *Jongmyo Jeryeak* is presented during the ritual reenactment.

Changdeokgung Palace was built in 1405, then burnt down in 1592 during the Japanese invasions and later rehabilitated. The palace itself is a masterful work but particularly noteworthy is its back garden called the *Huwon*, which is widely acclaimed for its beautifully landscaped and creative gardens. The garden, comprising some 300,000 square meters of the entire 405,636 square meters of the palace property, is tastefully laid out with picturesque pavilions and halls, lotus ponds, uniquely shaped rocks, stone bridges, stairways, water troughs and springs scattered among dense woods, all essential elements of a traditional Korean-style garden.

Hwaseong Fortress was constructed over 34 months in Suwon, south of Seoul, in 1796. Most of the 5,743-meter exterior fortress wall still remains. In 1997, UNESCO initiated a Memory of the World register for the purpose of preserving records and documents which opened new horizons of technology at the time of their creation.

Among Korea's written heritage, *Hunminjeongeum* and *Joseonwangjosillok* have been included on this register. *Hunminjeongeum* (proper phonetic system to instruct the people) was a primer for teaching *Hangeul*, the Korean alphabet created by the Joseon Dynasty's fourth ruler, King Sejong.

The new alphabet was promulgated during King Sejong's 28th year on the throne in 1446. *Joseonwangjosillok* (Annals of the Joseon Dynasty) resulted from the tradition of preparing a historical document for each reign, which began in 1413 with the Annals of King Taejo, the founder and first king of Joseon, and continued through the end of the dynasty.

The Annals were drafted by historians in the Office for Annals Compilation (*Chunchugwan*) and to ensure preservation, copies were stored in special repositories situated in different parts of the country. UNESCO said it registered Korean treasures as a way of sharing the excellent culture and heritage of Korea with the world.

Fine Arts

The oldest known examples of sculpture in Korea are rock carvings on a riverside cliff named *Bangudae* in Ulsan. In other parts of the country,

Gilt-bronze Maitreya (the Buddha of the future) of Goguryeo Kingdom(left), a gold crown of the Silla Kingdom (right)

clay, bone and stone figurines of men and animals have been excavated. In these Neolithic village sites, comb pattern pottery was the main art form of the period, which were replaced by curved designs with the advent of agriculture.

A few objects from prehistoric times have been found across Korea. Based on their abstract forms, they are presumed to have been created for religious purposes. A variety of bronze items were produced, but the traditions of the Neolithic Age lingered and art of this period continued to be closely linked with religion.

During the Three Kingdoms period, when a new social order was being shaped, Korean art was simple and robust. However, the flourishing of Buddhism enriched both the content and techniques of the art of that period. All the three kingdoms enthusiastically supported religion, and sculpted works from Goguryeo (37 B.C.- A.D. 668), Baekje (18 B.C.-A.D. 660) and Silla (57 B.C.-A.D. 935) that

The *Emille* Bell (late 8th century) is the largest of its kind in Korea.

were typically dominated by Buddhist images.

Prime examples include Goguryeo's gilt bronze standing *Tathagata Buddha* and the gilt bronze half-seated Maitreya in meditation, both of which are wearing benign smiles. Baekje statues, such as the stone Buddha carved on a cliff at Seosan, exhibit elegant facial contours and smiles, typical elements of Baekje art.

Although Unified Silla's art featured realistic techniques, it sought a flawless socio-political harmony. During this period, the art of metalcraft achieved a brilliant state of sophistication. From the large mounded tombs of Silla's aristocracy, archaeologists have uncovered rich collections of gold accessories of kings and queens, including crowns, earrings, necklaces and girdles.

The golden crowns in particular attest to a truly refined artistry. Linear engraving and repose work embellish the upright tree-shaped ornaments, the diadems, while the pendants are further decorated with gold spangles and comma-shaped jade attached with fine wire. Recovered earrings show a refined filigree combined with granulation.

Silla artisans also excelled in producing temple bells. The bronze bells are well-known for their elegant design, sonorous sound and impressive size.

The late eighth-century Divine Bell of King Seongdeok, or the *Emille* Bell as it is popularly known, is the largest of existing temple bells in Korea. It is decorated with exquisite sculpting of lotus-shaped medallions, flowers, flames and heavenly maidens.

Inlaid Celadon vase from the Goryeo Dynasty

The artistry of Goryeo (r. 918-1392) can be best appreciated by its celadon ware, with its beautiful color, particularly jade green, a wide variety of items —jars, wine pitchers, plates, cups, incense burners, and flower vases—and elegant decorations which are incised, carved in relief or inlaid. These celadon works, produced during the 12th and 13th centuries, were used for ostentatious display rather than for practical use. It may be said that this celadon ware embodied the yearning for a spiritual world beyond the mundane life.

Celadon techniques were brought to Goryeo from Song Dynasty China (r. 960-1279), but the Chinese influence was all but lost by the first half of the 12th century when Korean creativity came into full bloom. The technique of inlaying, devised by Korean potters, involved incising designs into the clay and then filling the recesses with white or black slip.

Excess slip was scraped away prior to firing. These designs, applied in a simple and restrained manner in the early stage, resulted in a subtle and dignified beauty for celadon vessels. By the end of the 13th

Blue and white Porcelain with Bamboo and Pinetree Design, the Joseon Dynasty

century, however, potters used these popular designs without restraint and craftsmanship deteriorated.

Inlaid designs became more coarse after the Mongol invasions. Celadon-making skills vanished in the 14th century, but have been revived by artisans of today. There are many people who have devoted their entire life and energy to reviving *Cheongja*, the blue-green celadon of Goryeo. What celadon was to Goryeo is what white porcelain was to Joseon. Ceramic artists of Joseon initially created *buncheong*, a grayish stoneware with white slip and greyish-green glaze, but then developed this into white porcelain over time.

The dominant social influence of Joseon was Confucianism. The shift from the leisurely aristocratic Goryeo period to the more pragmatic social concepts of Confucianism are reflected in the ceramic art of the time.

White porcelain opted for simple lines over the more curvy shapes of Goryeo celadon. During Joseon, the kilns were controlled by the government and produced inlaid white porcelain as well as inlaid blue celadon.

White porcelain in underglaze blue was usually decorated with patterns of *Sagunja* (four virtuous plants favored as traditional art symbols), including plum blossoms, orchids, chrysanthemums and bam-

Muryangsujeon, the oldest wooden structure in Korea

boo, lotus flowers, arabesque designs and autumn grass. Joseon porcelain is being actively researched and revived by dedicated ceramic artists of today.

Such potters' efforts to revive the arts of the bygone days can be observed in Icheon, a small town about an hour outside of Seoul.

Korea's architectural designs can be divided into two major styles according to the structures involved. For the designs used in palaces and temples, ancient Korean architects used a bracket system, while commoners's houses were characterized by thatched roofs and *ondol,* heated floors. The upper class usually built larger houses with tiled roofs, which were elegantly curved and accentuated with slightly uplifted eaves.

What came into the architect's mind was how to harmonize the subject structures with the natural surroundings. Among ancient architectural designs, Goryeo's wooden structure *Muryangsujeon* (Hall of Eternal Life) still stands at Buseoksa Temple in Yeongju, Gyeongsangbuk-do Province. It is presumed to have been built in the 13th century.

Western architecture was introduced to Korea at the end of the 19th century, as churches and offices for foreign legations were built by architects and engineers from abroad.

Since the 1960s, in Korea's pursuit of industrialization and urbanization, the government has pushed ahead with development plans and a number of beautiful old buildings have been demolished and replaced by unsightly structures.

However, in recent years, there have been active discussions in this regard while the time-honored concept of harmonizing buildings with nature is being revived.

Literature

Korean literature is usually divided chronologically into classical and modern periods. Korea's classical literature developed against the backdrop of traditional folk beliefs of the Korean people; it was also influenced by Taoism, Confucianism, and Buddhism. Among these, Buddhist influence held the greatest sway, followed by enormous influences from Confucianism during the Joseon period.

Modern literature in Korea, on the other hand, developed out of its contact with Western culture, following the course of modernization. Not only Christian thought, but also various artistic trends and influences were imported from the West. As the "New Education" and the "National Language and Literature Movement" developed, the Chinese writing system, which had traditionally represented the culture of the dominant class, lost the socio-cultural function it had previously enjoyed.

The *Hyangga* poetry of the Silla period signaled

the beginning of a unique poetic form in Korean literature. The *Hyangga* were recorded in the *hyangchal* script, in which the Korean language was written using "sound" (*eum*) and "meaning" (*hun*) of Chinese characters. Fourteen poems in the *Hyangga* style from the Silla period have been preserved in the *Samgungnyusa* (Memorabilia of the Three Kingdoms).

The literature of the Goryeo period is marked by an increased use of Chinese letters, the disappearance of Hyangga, and the emergence of *Goryeogayo* (Goryeo songs) which continued to be transmitted as oral literature until the Joseon period.

The creation of the Korean alphabet, *Hangeul*, in the early Joseon period was one of the turning points in the history of Korean literature. *Akjang* (musical scores) was written in the Korean script, such as *Yongbieocheonga* (Songs of Flying Dragons Through the Heavens).

The *sijo* (current tune) is representative of Joseon period poetry. Its poetic form was established in the late Goryeo period, but it flourished to a greater extent under the Joseon period's new leading ideology, Song Neo-Confucianism. As another form of the Joseon period poetry, the *gasa* is properly placed in the category of verse, but its content is not limited to the expression of individual sentiment. It often includes moral admonitions.

The first classical fictions in Korea include Kim Si-seup's *Geumosinhwa* (Tales of Geumo) which was written in Chinese characters and Heo Gyun's *Honggildongjeon* (Tales of Hong Gil-dong) written in *Hangeul*.

As time passed, the Korean script, *Hangeul*, was used widely in Korean society, resulting in the

A hunting scene from a sixth century Goguryeo tomb

growth and development of Korea language and literature studies.

Korean modern literature was formed against the background of the crumbling feudalistic society of the Joseon Dynasty, and the importation of new ideas from the West.

As forms of Korean modern literature, the *changga* (new type of song) and the *sinchesi* (new poetry) were hailed as the new poetic forms.

Painting

Korean painting represents the creative vigor and aesthetic sense of the Korean people.

Korean painting has developed steadily throughout its long history from the Three Kingdoms period (57 B.C.-A.D. 668) to modern times.

The best known paintings of the Three Kingdoms period are the murals in the old tombs of Goguryeo,

134

painted on the four walls and the ceiling of the burial chamber. While Goguryeo paintings were dynamic and rhythmic, the paintings of Silla were more meditative and meticulous. Silla's art bloomed after the unified Three Kingdoms in the 7th century.

Seodang, a private elementary school, by Kim Hong-do (1745-1806)

In the Goryeo period (r. 918-1392), painting flourished in great variety, inheriting the artistic tradition of Unified Silla which marked the golden age of painting. Artists of the era created temple murals and Buddhist scroll paintings, marking a flourishing Korean Buddhism.

During the Joseon era, professional painters usually produced landscapes at the request of noble families. It was in the late 18th century that painters turned to the everyday life of people, probably under the influence of the *Silhak* (Practical Studies) movement following the Catholic missionaries introduction of European science and technology into Korea. Paintings with secular themes formed a new trend known as "genre painting".

Kim Hong-do filled his canvas with scenes from the daily lives of the gentry, farmers, artisans and merchants. His precise but humorous depictions of subjects expressed the traditional Korean character.

"Imha-tuho-do," depicting a game of arrow-throwing, painted by Shin Yoon-bok (1758-?)

Paintings by anonymous artists, though less sophisticated in style than those by Confucian artist-scholars, dealt more with the daily life of common people and their aspirations and dreams. These paintings featured vivid colors and were free of conventional restraints.

Following Japan's forcible annexation of Korea in 1910, the traditional styles of painting were gradually overshadowed by Western oil painting styles that were introduced during that period and later became prevalent. After Korea's liberation from Japan's rule in 1945, the tradition of Korean painting was revived by a number of outstanding artists, whereas many Korean artists educated in Europe and the United States helped their home country keep up with the contemporary trends of the outside world.

In the 1950s, a government-run institution, the National Exhibition played a leading role in the advancement of Korean art. The National Exhibition

The art world of Paik Nam-june, the renowned video-artist.

had a rather formal and academic atmosphere, tended to choose works that were realistic. Young artists pursuing creativity in their works, therefore, sought an art in tune with the new age. From the late 1960s, modern Korean painting began to change its directions to geometrical abstraction. Other artists took a deep interest in subject matters that conveyed the innate unity between man and nature.

Korean paintings of the 1980s were largely a reaction to the modernism of the 1970s. During this period, artists strongly felt that art should convey a message dealing with current social issues. Since then, there has been an interest in the issues of modernism and post-modernism.

In 1995, the International Gwangju Biennale was held in Gwangju, the capital of Jeollanam-do. The event provided an opportunity for modern Korean artists to get together in one place with leading figures from the international art world. Paik Nam-june's video art was one of the most prominent exhibitions.

In Korea today, both traditional and Western-style painting are taught and pursued, producing one of the most versatile communities of fine arts in the world. Many Korean painters are active in New York, Paris and other centers of contemporary art.

Music and Dance

Music and dance were means of religious worship and this tradition continued through the Three Kingdoms period.

More than 30 musical instruments were used during the Three Kingdoms period, and particularly noteworthy was the *hyeonhakgeum* (black crane zither), which Wang San-ak of Goguryeo created by altering the seven-string zither of Jin Dynasty China. Also notable was the *gayageum* (zither of Gaya), which was used in Gaya (r. 42-562) and brought to Silla by Ureuk. The 12-string *gayageum* is still played in modern Korea.

Goryeo followed the musical tradition of Silla in its early years, but came to have more diversified genres later. There were three types of music in Goryeo — *Dangak*, meaning music from Tang Dynasty China, *hyangak* or village music, and *aak* or court music. Some Goryeo music was inherited by Joseon and is still used in ceremonies today, especially those involving ancestral worship.

As in music, Goryeo enjoyed the dance tradition of Three Kingdoms initially, but later added more varieties with the introduction of court and religious dance from China's Song Dynasty.

During the Joseon Dynasty period, music was respected as an important element of rituals and ceremonies. Early in the dynasty, two offices dealing with musical matters were established and efforts were made to arrange musical texts.

As a result, a canon of music called *Akhakgwe-beom* was produced in 1493. The book classified music to be played at court into three categories - ceremonial music, Chinese music and native songs. Especially during King Sejong's reign, scores of musical instruments were newly developed. In addition to court music, the traditions of secular music such as *dangak* and *hyangak* continued.

Folk dance, including the farmers' dance, shaman dance and monk dance, became popular in the later days of Joseon, along with the masked dance known as *sandaenori* and puppet dance.

Masked dance, which combined dance with song and narrative, included shamanistic elements and thus greatly appealed to the grassroots. The performance was often accented by satirical passages that mocked the nobility, which the commoner audiences enjoyed all the more.

As for traditional dance, Confucian and Buddhist influences were very prominent. Confucian influence was often repressive, while Buddhism allowed a more tolerant attitude as shown in the beautiful court dances and many shaman dances for the dead.

A large number of traditional dances withered away during Japan's colonial rule, as well as the rapid industrialization and urbanization of Korea in the 1960s and 1970s. It was in the 1980s that people began to think about reviving these long-forgotten dances. Of the 56 original court dances, only a few are well-known today.

They include *Cheoyongmu* (Mask Dance) of Silla, *Hakchum* (Crane Dance) of Goryeo, and

A performance of *Aak*, court music

Chunaengjeon (Nightingale-singing-in-the-spring Dance) of Joseon. All of these dances have been designated as "Intangible Cultural Properties" by the government for their perpetuation while professional performers have been granted the titles of "Human Cultural Assets," the highest honor awarded to masters of traditional arts and crafts.

The development of modern dance in Korea was due largely to such pioneers as Jo Taek-won and Choe Seung-hui who were active during the Japanese colonial period. Following liberation, the Seoul Ballet Company was founded in 1950 to become the first organization that staged performances of ballet and modern dance.

Western music was first heard in Korea with the introduction of a Christian hymnal in 1893, and began to be taught at schools in 1904. *Changga*, a new type of song sung to Western melodies, flourished across the country.

As the nation experienced tumultuous changes with its forced opening to the West and the prolonged Japanese colonial rule, changga was sung to enhance

Vocalist Jo Su-mi, Conductor-pianist Chung Myung-whun

Korea's love of nation, spirit of independence, and new education and culture. In 1919, Hong Nanpa composed *Bongseonhwa* (Touch-me-not) in the form of *changga*.

After national liberation in 1945, Korea's first Western-style orchestra was inaugurated as the Korea Philharmonic Orchestra Society. Today there are nearly 50 full orchestras in Seoul and the provinces.

An increasing number of Korean musicians are performing outside Korea these days, winning acclaim from concert audiences and awards at prestigious international competitions. Among the most notable performers are the Chung Trio conductor-pianist Chung Myung-whun, cellist Chung Myung-wha and violinist Chung Kyung-wha.

Among singers, sopranos Jo Su-mi, Shin Young-ok and Hong Hye-gyong have all established an impressive presence in the international community of music. They have performed leading roles in productions at New York's Metropolitan Opera and other famed stages in addition to recording for world-famous music companies.

The musical "The Last Empress"

In August 1997, "The Last Empress," a musical depicting the last years of Korea's monarchy and Empress *Myeongseong*, was staged in New York to the wide acclaim of the American press. The musical, an epic tale, was viewed as offering a precious opportunity to expose Korean history and culture to Americans, particularly Korean-Americans.

To preserve and further develop traditional Korean music and performing arts, the National Center for Korean Traditional Performing Arts was established in 1951. The government established the Korean National University of Arts in 1993 to offer world class education in the arts and to cultivate professional artists. The University has six institutes — Music, Drama, Dance, Visual Arts, Film & Multimedia and Korean Traditional Arts. The Schools of Music and Dance are located in Seocho-dong, while the others are in Seokgwan-dong.

Drama and Movies

Korean drama has its origins in prehistoric religious rites, while music and dance play an integral role in all traditional theatrical performances. A good example of this classical theatrical form is the masked dance called *sandaenori* or *talchum*, a combination of dance, song and narrative punctuated with satire and humor. Slightly varying from one region to another in terms of style, dialogue and costume, it enjoyed remarkable popularity among rural people until the early 20th century.

Pansori, the lengthy narrative songs based on popular tales, and *kkokdugaksinoreum* or puppet plays, performed by vagabond artists, also drew large audiences. The shamanistic rituals known as *gut* were another form of religious theater that appealed to the populace. All these performances are presented nowadays, too, though not very often.

There are a few institutions that offer various performing arts in one place, an example of this being Jeong-dong Theater in central Seoul, that presents a traditional performing arts series, drama and music.

The first performance of *singeuk* (new drama), a departure from the masked dance and other forms of traditional dramas, was presented in December 1902. However, modern drama began to take firm root in the 1910s after the first Western-style theater was opened in Seoul in 1908. The theater named *Wongaksa* was in operation until November 1909.

Theatrical groups *Hyeoksindan* and *Munsuseong* were also organized by those who returned from study in Japan and staged *sinpa* (new wave) dramas. *Sinpa* was a concept that countered *gupa* (old wave) drama, meaning *kabuki* of Japan. *Sinpa* dramas first dealt with political and military themes and then diversified into detective stories, soap operas and tragedies.

While sinpa dramas proved to be a passing fad, a

A performance of *Pansori*, dramatic narrative song

genuine new wave of dramas was promoted by artists who rallied around *Wongaksa* and raised the curtain of modern drama. In 1922, *Towolhoe*, a coterie of theatrical figures, was formed, with this organization leading the drama movement across the country, staging as many as 87 performances. Drama remained popular until the 1930s, but then subsided in the socio-political turmoil of the 1940s and '50s. In the following decade, it was further weakened amidst the boom of motion pictures and the emergence of television.

In the 1970s, a number of young artists began to study and adopt the styles and themes of traditional theatrical works like the masked dance plays, shaman rituals and *pansori*. The Korean Culture and Arts Foundation has been sponsoring an annual drama festival to encourage local theatrical performances. At present, a great number of theatrical groups are active all the year round, featuring all manner of genres from comedy to historical epics at small theaters along Daehangno Street in downtown Seoul. Some theatrical performances become very successful and are staged for extended runs.

The first Korean-made film was shown to the public in 1919. Entitled "Righteous Revenge," it was a so-called kino-drama designed to be combined with a stage performance. The first feature film, "Oath Under the Moon," was screened in 1923. In 1926, charismatic actor-director Na Un-gyu drew an enthusiastic response from the public by producing "Arirang," a cinematic protest against Japanese oppression.

After the Korean War in 1953, the local film industry grew gradually and enjoyed a booming business for about a decade. But the next two decades saw a stagnation of the industry due largely to the rapid growth of television. Since the early 1980s, however, the film industry has regained some vitality thanks mainly to a few talented young directors who boldly discarded old stereotypes in movie making.

Their efforts succeeded and their movies have earned recognition at various international festivals including Cannes, Chicago, Berlin, Venice, London, Tokyo, Moscow and other cities. This positive trend has been accelerating in the 1990s with more and more Korean directors producing movies that have moved the hearts of world citizens based on unique Korean experiences and sentiments.

In 2000, *Chunhyangjeon* (the story of Chunhyang), directed by Im Kwon-taek, became the first Korean film to compete in the Cannes Film Festival. Four other films were screened in non-competitive categories. The film *Seom* (Island), directed by Kim Ki-duk, competed in the Venice International Film Festival.

Following these films, in 2001, Joint Security Area was selected to compete in the Berlin International

Scenes from the movie "Shiri," directed by Kang Je-kyu, "The Tale of Chunhyang," a movie directed by Im Kwon-taek.

Film Festival and another film by Kim Ki-duk, Address Unknown entered the competition section of the Venice International Film Festival.

Public interest in films has been mounting and several international film festivals have been staged by provincial governments or private organizations in Korea. They include the Busan International Film Festival, the Bucheon International Fantastic Film Festival, the Jeonju International Film Festival and the Women's Film Festival in Seoul.

As in other countries, Korean cinema circles are seeing a noticeable expansion of the animation and cartoon industry. More than 200 companies are producing works in this up-to-date genre.

The film, video, animation and on-line content industries are also undergoing a boom in Korea, fueled by the availability of high-speed Internet services.

In 2001, Korea's film industry experienced great success at the box office. The market share of local films was over 46% due to several Korean blockbusters, including Friends which broke box-office records, My Sassy Girl and Kick the Moon. Korea released 237 films with a combined production value of about US$11.2 million. Movie houses showed 52 Korean-made films.

Museums and Theaters

Korea abounds in cultural facilities of all levels and categories where people can enjoy exhibitions and stage performances throughout the year. These places offer an on-the-spot glimpse into the cultural and artistic achievements of Koreans past and present, regarding both traditional and modern trends and tastes.

From full-scale museums of international standards to small theaters where performers and spectators can casually mingle and interact, these facilities vary in type and scale so as to satisfy the diverse interests and penchants of their target audiences.

There are 289 museums in Korea, with ten being funded and operated by the central government, including the National Museum of Korea and the National Folk Museum located in downtown Seoul. Others are located in provincial cities, some of which were the capitals of ancient kingdoms. In particular, Gyeongju and Buyeo are treasure houses of historic remains and relics that reveal the cultural brilliance of their respective region. As such, each museum features a unique historical flavor.

In addition to the national and public museums as well as college and university museums, there are more than 140 private museums in Korea that have been established by private citizens, religious organizations and business enterprises.

In most cases, their collections consist of cultural

National Museum of Contemporary Art

artifacts which involved a lifetime of dedicated efforts to gather. The collections range from folk paintings, books, religious objects, furniture and embroidery to traditional costumes.

In recent years, museums with unusual collections have appeared including a museum specializing in *kimchi*, Korea's trademark pickled cabbage and radish.

Korea has about 80 multi-purpose theaters. The National Theater, founded in 1950, is located at the foot of Mt. Namsan in the heart of Seoul. With a goal of preserving and developing traditional culture and contemporary performing arts, it has gone through a half century of hardship and change and is now rightfully proud of its four resident companies who stage some 35 regular productions annually.

The four include the National Drama Company, National *Changgeuk* (Korean musical drama) Company, National Dance Company and National Traditional Music Orchestra. These companies frequently present special tour performances overseas and across Korea. Besides the four resident compa-

Opera House at the Seoul Arts Center

nies, three others were quite active — The National Opera Company, The National Ballet Company and The National Chorus. These three were reborn as independently-run companies residing at the Seoul Arts Center in Feb, 2000.

The National Museum of Contemporary Art, located in a scenic park south of Seoul, features an extensive collection of Korean and Western art works of the 20th century.

The number of art galleries has greatly increased in the past two decades amid growing public interest in fine art. Galleries of varied size and character are clustered in such areas as Insa-dong, downtown Seoul, which is dubbed "Mary's Alley" by resident foreigners, Sagan-dong near *Gyeongbokgung* Palace, and Cheongdam-dong, southern Seoul.

One of Korea's largest multi-purpose theater is the Sejong Center for the Performing Arts, located in the center of Seoul. Affiliated with this municipal arts center, opened in 1978, are the Seoul Philharmonic Orchestra, the Seoul Metropolitan Korean Traditional Music Orchestra, the Seoul Metropolitan Choir, the

Seoul Metropolitan Theater Company, the Seoul Metropolitan Musical Company, the Seoul Metropolitan Dance Company, the Seoul Metropolitan Opera Company, the Seoul Metropolitan Boys and Girls Choir and the Seoul Youth Philharmonic Orchestra. The center's main hall can seat 3,800, while its pipe organ is one of the finest in the world.

The Seoul Arts Center, located in southern Seoul, is Korea's first multi-disciplinary art center and cultural center in Korea. The Center, covering a total land area of over 234,385 square meters and a total floor space of 120,951 square meters, opened in three stages from 1988 to 1993.

With its beautiful architecture, the Opera House has three separate theaters. The Opera Theater, 2,278 seats, is equipped to host grand operas, ballets and more. Towol Theater, 669 seats, is a medium-sized theater for plays, smaller-scale operas and modern dance.

The Jayu Theater, which can accommodate a maximum of 350 seats, is for experimental and avant-garde performances. The Concert Hall, 2,600 seats, is a large hall for full orchestras, while the Recital Hall, 380 seats, is for solo or chamber orchestras. And the Center has an Art Gallery, Calligraphy Hall, Arts Library, Open-air Theater and Film Archive.

Since its completion, Seoul Arts Center has been recognized by artists from a number of disciplines as an unique place for fostering, promoting and staging creative works. As a world-class institution, the Seoul Arts Center now play a role in leading Korean culture into the next century.

Korean Lifestyle

It is generally surmised that Paleolithic man began to inhabit the Korean Peninsula about 40,000 to 50,000 years ago, although it has yet to be confirmed if they were the ethnic ancestors of present-day Koreans. Some Paleolithic men lived in caves, while others built structures on level ground. They lived on fruit and edible roots and by hunting and fishing.

Neolithic man appeared in Korea around 4000 B.C., with signs of their active presence around 3000 B.C. being found across the peninsula. It is believed that the Neolithic people formed the ethnic stock of the Korean people. Neolithic people dwelled near the seashore and riverbanks before advancing into inland areas. The sea was their main source of food. They used nets, hooks and fishing lines to catch fish and gather shellfish. Hunting was another way to procure food. Arrowheads and spear points have been found at Neolithic sites. Later, they began to engage in farming using stone hoes, sickles and millstones.

Rice cultivation started during the Bronze Age, generally thought to have lasted in Korea until around 400 B.C. People also lived in pits, while dolmen and stone cist tombs were used predominantly for burials during the period.

As agriculture became a principal activity, villages were formed and a ruling leader emerged along with supreme authority. Law became necessary to govern the communities. In Gojoseon (2333 B.C.-194 B.C.), a law code consisting of eight articles came into

Korean traditional house with *giwa*, black-grooved tiles for the roof

practice, but only three of the articles are known today. They are as follows: First, anybody who kills another shall immediately be killed. Second, those who injures another's body shall compensate in grain. Third, those who steals other's possessions shall become a slave of his victim.

Traditional Korean houses remained relatively unchanged from the Three Kingdoms period through the late Joseon Dynasty (1392-1910).

Ondol, a unique Korean under-floor heating system, was first used in the north. Smoke and heat were channeled through flues built under the floor. In the warmer south, *ondol* was used together with wooden floors. The major materials of traditional houses were clay and wood. *Giwa*, or black-grooved tiles for roof, were made of earth, usually red clay. Today, the presidential mansion is called *Cheong Wa Dae*, or Blue House, after the blue tiles used for its roof.

Traditional houses were built without using any

nails but rather assembled with wooden pegs. Upper-class houses consisted of a number of separate structures, one for accommodation of women and children, one for the men of the family and their guests, and another for servants, all enclosed within a wall. A family ancestral shrine was built behind the house. A lotus pond was sometimes created in front of the house outside the wall.

The form of the houses differed from the colder north to the warmer south. Simple houses with a rectangular floor and a kitchen and a room on either side developed into an L-shaped house in the south, but would become U-shaped or square-shaped with a courtyard at the center in the north.

From the late 1960s, Korea's housing pattern began to change rapidly with the construction of Western-style apartment buildings. High-rise apartments have mushroomed all over the country since the 1970s.

Koreans began to weave cloth with hemp and arrowroot and raised silkworms to produce silk. During the Three Kingdoms period, men wore *jeogori* (jacket), *baji* (trousers), and *durumagi* (overcoat) complete with a hat, belt and pair of shoes. The women wore *jeogori* (short jacket) with two long ribbons which are tied to form an *otgoreum* knot, a full length, high-waist wrap-around skirt called *chima*, a *durumagi*, complete with *beoseon*, white cotton socks, and boat-shaped shoes. This attire, known as *hanbok*, has been handed down in the same form for men and women for hundreds of years with little change except for the length of the *jeogori* and *chima*.

Western wear entered Korea during the Korean War (1950-53), and during the rapid industrialization in the 1960s and 1970s, *hanbok* use declined, being

Korean traditional costume

regarded as inappropriate for casual wear. Recently, however, *hanbok* lovers have been campaigning to revitalize *hanbok*, and have created updated styles which are easier to wear.

Traditional *hanbok* is usually worn on special days like the lunar New Year holidays and *Chuseok* (Autumnal Full Moon Harvest Festival), and family festivities such as *Hwangap*, which marks one's 60th birthday.

Of the three basic elements of life — house, clothing and food — the change in dietary habits has most significantly affected Koreans. Rice still remains the staple of most Koreans, but among the younger generations, many prefer Western-style food.

Rice has been usually accompanied by various side

Housewives making *Kimchi*, Korea's famous red-pepper cabbage dish.

dishes, mostly seasoned vegetables, soup, pot stew, and meat.

A traditional Korean meal is not complete without *kimchi*, a mixture of various pickled vegetables such as Oriental cabbage, radish, green onion and cucumber. Certain types of *kimchi* are made spicy with the addition of red pepper powder, while others are prepared without red peppers or are soaked in a tasty liquid. However, garlic is always used in *kimchi* to add to its flavor.

In late November or early December, Korean families engage in *gimjang*, or preparation of *kimchi*, for the long winter season. Until a few decades ago, the *kimchi* prepared for the winter was placed into large vessels which were stored underground to retain the flavor of the *kimchi*. With the emergence of apartment houses, electronic appliance makers are now manufacturing refrigeration units exclusively for *kimchi*. In addition, *kimchi* factories enjoy a brisk business as an increasing number of families buy *kimchi* instead of preparing it themselves.

In addition to *kimchi*, *doenjang* (Korean bean

Korean Traditional full-course dinner

paste), with its anti-cancer attributes, has attracted the attention of modern-day nutritionists. Koreans used to make *doenjang* at home by boiling yellow beans, drying them in the shade, soaking them in salty water, and fermenting them in sunlight. However, only a few families go through this process at home these days while the majority buy factory-made *doenjang*.

Among meat dishes, seasoned *bulgogi* (usually beef) and *galbi* (beef or pork rib) are most favored by both Koreans and foreigners.

Family Life

In traditional Korea, the typical family was large with three or four generations usually living together. Because infant mortality was high and a big family was thought of as a blessing, having many children was desired. However, the rapid industrialization and urbanization of the country in the 1960s and 1970s were accompanied by an effective birth control drive, and the average number of children in a family has been dramatically decreased to two or less in the

1980s.

Having a long Confucian tradition under which the eldest son takes over as head of the family, a preference for sons was prevalent in Korea. To tackle the problem of male preference, the government has completely rewritten family-related laws in a way that ensures equality for sons and daughters in terms of inheritance.

Industrialization of the country has made life more hectic and complicated. Young married couples have begun to separate from their extended families and start their own homes. Now almost all families are couple-centered nuclear families.

Names

Korean names have almost invariably consisted of three Chinese characters that are pronounced with three Korean syllables. The family name comes first, while the remaining two characters form the given name.

However, this old tradition no longer remains intact. Of course, the majority still follow this tradition, but more and more people make their children's names in pure Korean words that cannot be written in Chinese characters.

But the family names remain unchanged in most cases. Changes are more varied for given names.

There are about 300 family names in Korea, but only a handful make up the vast majority of the population. Among the most common names are Kim, Lee, Pak or Park, An, Jang, Jo or Cho, Choe or Choi, Jong or Cheong, Han, Gang or Kang, Yu or Yoo and Yun or Yoon.

Korean women do not change their family name upon marriage. When Americans call a woman Mrs.

Smith that means she is the wife of a man named Smith. In Korea, when a married woman says she is Mrs. Kim, it usually means that her surname at birth was Kim.

Some women call themselves by their husbands' family names but this is very rare. Koreans do not refer to others by their given names except among very close friends. Even among siblings, the younger ones are not supposed to address their elders by given names but rather *eonni*, meaning elder sister, or *oppa*, meaning elder brother.

Festivals

In bygone days, festivals were lavish religious observances. It was during the Confederated Kingdoms period that harvest thanksgiving festivals began to be observed officially. They included the *yeonggo* (spirit-invoking drums) of Buyeo, *dong-maeng* (worship of the founder) of Goguryeo, and *mucheon* (dance to Heaven) of Dongye. Usually, fes-

A family making *Songpyeon*, half moon-shaped rice cakes for *Chuseok*.

tivals were conducted in the tenth month, according to the lunar calendar, after harvests were over, with the exception of *yeonggo* on the 12th month.

The tradition of enjoying the autumnal harvest and greeting the new year in merriment continued through the later kingdoms and dynasties, although each kingdom had its addition and deletion of holidays. Due to the hectic pace of life today, modern Korea has lost many of its traditional holidays.

But a few holidays are still celebrated fervently. One such day is *Seol*, the first day of a year by the lunar calendar, which falls sometime in late January to late February by the Western calendar. The entire family gathers on that day.

Dressed mostly in *hanbok* or their best outfits, the family observes ancestral rites. After the ceremonies, the younger members make a traditional deep bow to their elders.

Other major holidays include *Daeboreum*, the first full moon of the year after *Seol*. During this holiday, farmers and fishermen pray for a bountiful harvest and catch, and ordinary households express yearning for a fortuitous year and the prevention of bad luck by preparing special dishes of seasonal vegetables.

On *Dano*, the fifth day of the fifth lunar month, farmers took a day off from the field for joint festivities marking the completion of sowing, while women washed their hair in special water prepared by boiling iris with the hope of preventing misfortune. *Dano* was a major holiday in the old days, but interest has decreased except in a few provinces.

Chuseok, the autumnal full moon day that falls on the 15th day of the eighth month by the lunar calendar, is probably the most anticipated festive day for modern Koreans.

Endless throngs of cars fill expressways and almost

Dol, the first birthday celebration

all institutions and stores are closed for three days. Family members get together, pay tribute to their ancestors, and visit ancestral graves. People living in cities return to their hometowns to observe *Chuseok*. Airplane and train tickets for those returning to their hometowns are usually reserved several months in advance.

Among other festive days are Buddha's Birthday, which falls on the eighth day of the fourth lunar month, and Christmas which not only Christians but most young people enjoy. On Buddha's Birthday, a huge crowd of Buddhists parade through the heart of Seoul, while lotus-shaped Buddhist lanterns are hung along major streets.

There are several family holidays that are important for all Koreans and that are celebrated with feasting and merriment.

They include *baegil*, the 100th day after a child's birth, *dol*, baby's first birthday, and *hoegap* or *hwangap*, one's 60th birthday, which is considered as the completion of the 60-year cycle of the Oriental zodiac. These special days were observed with much enthusiasm when infant mortality was high and life expectancy was low.

Such occasions were observed as festivals in which even remote relatives attended, but these days they are usually observed by only close family members. As for *hoegap*, more and more senior citizens turn to other forms of celebration such as overseas travel, instead of enjoying celebrations at home.

National Holidays

Date		
1/1	New Year's Day	The first day of the New Year is a public holiday.
	Seol	The first day of the first month by the lunar calendar: two days around this day are public holidays.
3/1	Independence Movement Day	This day marks the day when a large-scale independence movement was waged against Japanese colonial rule in 1919.
4/5	Arbor Day	A day when trees are planted throughout the country.
5/5	Children's Day	A day of various celebrations for children.
	Buddha's Birthday	The eighth day of the fourth month by the lunar calendar. Solemn rituals are held at Buddhist temples. The day's festivities are climaxed by a lantern parade in downtown Seoul.
6/6	Memorial Day	The nation pays tribute to its war dead. Memorial services are held at the National Cemetery.
7/17	Constitution Day	This day commemorates the promulgation of the Republic of Korea's Constitution in 1948.
8/15	Liberation Day	On this day in 1945, Korea was liberated from Japan's 35-year-long colonial rule. The day also marks the establishment of the government of the Republic of Korea in 1948.
	Chuseok	The 15th day of the eighth month by the lunar calendar. This is one of the biggest national holidays of the year. Families hold memorial services at home or at family graves. Viewing the full moon and making a wish is an important feature of the evening.
10/3	National Foundation Day	This day marks the founding of the first nation of Korea by Dangun in 2333 B.C.
12/25	Christmas Day	Both Christians and non-Christians alike celebrate this day, as in the West.

Religion

Unlike some cultures where a single religion is dominant, Korean culture includes a wide variety of religious elements that have shaped the people's way of thinking and behavior. In the early stages of history in Korea, religious and political functions were combined but later became distinct.

Historically, Koreans lived under the influences of shamanism, Buddhism, Taoism or Confucianism, and in modern times, the Christian faith has made strong inroads into the country, bringing forth yet another important factor that may change the spiritual landscape of the people. The rapid pace of industrialization which occurred within a couple of decades compared to a couple of centuries in the West, has brought about considerable anxiety and alienation while disrupting the peace of mind of Koreans, encouraging their pursuit of solace in religious activities. As a result, the population of religious believers has expanded markedly with religious institutions emerging as influential social organizations.

Freedom of religion is guaranteed by the Constitution in Korea. According to a 1995 social statistics survey, 50.7 percent of Koreans follow a specific religious faith. Buddhists account for some 46 percent followed by Protestants at 39 percent and Catholics at 13 percent of the religious population.

Shamanism

Shamanism is a primitive religion which does not have a systematic structure but permeates into the daily lives of the people through folklore and customs. Neolithic man in Korea had animistic beliefs that every object in the world possessed a soul.

Man was also believed to have a soul that never dies. So a corpse was laid with its head toward the east in the direction of the sunrise. Neolithic man believed that while good spirits like the sun would bring good luck to human beings, evil spirits would bring misfortune.

Shamanism gradually gave way to Confucianism or Buddhism as a tool for governing the people but its influence lingered on. The shaman, *Mudang* in Korean, is an intermediary who can link the living with the spiritual world where the dead reside. The shaman is considered capable of averting bad luck, curing sickness and assuring a propitious passage from this world to the next. The shaman is also believed to resolve conflicts and tensions that might exist between the living and the dead.

Korean shamanism includes the worship of thousands of spirits and demons that are believed to dwell in every object in the natural world, including rocks, trees, mountains and streams as well as celestial bodies.

Shamanism in ancient Korea was a religion of fear and superstition, but for modern generations, it remains a colorful and artistic ingredient of their culture. A shamanistic ritual, rich with exorcist elements, presents theatrical elements with music and dance.

The introduction of more sophisticated religions like Taoism, Confucianism and Buddhism did not result in the abandonment of shamanistic beliefs and practices. They assimilated elements of shamanistic faith and coexisted peacefully. Shamanism has remained an underlying religion of the Korean people as well as a vital aspect of their culture.

Buddhism

Buddhism is a highly disciplined philosophical religion which emphasizes personal salvation through rebirth in an endless cycle of reincarnation.

Buddhism was introduced into Korea in A.D. 372 during the Goguryeo Kingdom period by a monk named Sundo who came from Qian Qin Dynasty China. In 384, monk Malananda brought Buddhism to Baekje from the Eastern Jin State of China. In Silla, Buddhism was disseminated by a monk Ado of Goguryeo by the mid-fifth century. Buddhism seems to have been well supported by the ruling people of the Three Kingdoms because it was suitable as a spiritual prop for the governing structure, with Buddha as the single object of worship like the king as the single object of authority.

Under royal patronage, many temples and monasteries were constructed and believers grew steadily. By the sixth century monks and artisans were migrating to Japan with scriptures and religious artifacts to form the basis of early Buddhist culture there.

By the time Silla unified the peninsula in 668, it had embraced Buddhism as the state religion, though the government systems were along Confucian lines. Royal preference for Buddhism in this period produced a magnificent flowering for Buddhist arts and temple architecture including Bulguksa Temple and other relics in Gyeongju, the capital of Silla. The state cult of Buddhism began to deteriorate as the

Celebrating Buddha's birthday

nobility indulged in a luxurious lifestyle. Buddhism then established the *Seon* sect (zen) to concentrate on finding universal truth through a life of frugality.

The rulers of the succeeding Goryeo Dynasty were even more enthusiastic in their support of the religion. During Goryeo, Buddhist arts and architecture continued to flourish with unreserved support from the aristocracy. The *Tripitaka Koreana* was produced during this period. When Yi Seong-gye, founder of the Joseon Dynasty, staged a revolt and had himself proclaimed king in 1392, he tried to remove all influences of Buddhism from the government and adopted Confucianism as the guiding principles for state management and moral decorum. Throughout the five-century reign of Joseon, any effort to revive Buddhism was met with strong opposition from Confucian scholars and officials.

When Japan forcibly took over Joseon as a colonial ruler in 1910, he made attempts to assimilate Korean Buddhist sects with those of Japan. These attempts however failed and even resulted in a revival of interest in native Buddhism among Koreans. The past few decades have seen Buddhism undergo a sort of renaissance involving efforts to adapt to the changes of modern society. While the majority of monks remain in mountainous areas, absorbed in self-discipline and meditation, some come down to the cities to spread their religion. There are a large number of monks indulging in scholastic research in religion at universities in and outside Korea. *Seon* (meditation)-oriented Korean Buddhism has been growing noticeably with many foreigners following in the footsteps of revered Korean monks through training at *Songgwangsa* temple in Jeollanam-do province and *Seon* centers in Seoul and provincial cities.

Confucianism

Confucianism was the moral and religious belief founded by Confucius in the 6th century B.C. Basically it is a system of ethical percepts - benevolent love, righteousness, decorum and wise leadership - designed to inspire and preserve the good management of family and society.

Confucianism was a religion without a god like early Buddhism, but ages passed and the sage and principal disciplines were canonized by late followers.

Confucianism was introduced along with the earliest specimens of Chinese written materials around the beginning of the Christian era. The Three Kingdoms of Goguryeo, Baekje and Silla all left records that indicate the early existence of Confucian influence. In Goguryeo, a state university called *Daehak* was established in 372 and private Confucian academies were founded in the province. Baekje set up such institutions even earlier.

The Unified Silla sent delegations of scholars to

A Confucius ritual

Tang China to observe the workings of the Confucian institutions firsthand and to bring back voluminous writings on the subjects. For Goryeo Dynasty in the 10th century, Buddhism was the state religion, and Confucianism formed the philosophical and structural backbone of the state. The civil service examination of *Gwageo*, adopted after the Chinese system in the late 10th century, greatly encouraged studies in the Confucian classics and deeply implanted Confucian values in Korean minds.

The Joseon Dynasty, which was established in 1392, accepted Confucianism as the official ideology and developed a Confucian system of education, ceremony and civil administration. When Korea was invaded by many West European countries including Japan in the late 19th century, the Confucianists raised "righteous armies" to fight against the aggressor. Efforts were also made to reform Confucianism to adapt it to the changing conditions of the times.

These reformists accepted the new Western civilization and endeavored to establish a Modern Independence government. Also, during Japan's colonial rule of Korea, these reformists joined many independence movements to fight against imperial Japan. Today, Confucian ancestral worship is still prevalent and filial piety highly revered as a virtue in Korean society.

Catholicism

The tide of Christian mission activity reached Korea in the 17th century, when copies of Catholic missionary Matteo Ricci's works in Chinese were brought from Beijing by the annual tributary mission to the Chinese Emperor. Along with religious doctrine, these books included aspects of Western learning such as the solar calendar and other matters that attracted the attention of the Joseon scholars of *Silhak*, or the School of Practical Learning.

By the 18th century, there were several converts among these scholars and their families. No priests entered Korea until 1794, when a Chinese priest Zhou wenmo visited Korea. The number of converts continued to increase, although the propagation of foreign religion on Korean soil was still technically against the law and there were sporadic persecutions. By the year 1865, a dozen priests presided over a community of some 23,000 believers.

With the coming to power in 1863 of Daewongun, a xenophobic prince regent, persecution began in earnest and continued until 1873. In 1925, 79 Koreans who had been martyred during the Joseon Dynasty persecutions were beatified at St. Peter's Basilica in Rome, and in 1968 an additional 24 were honored in the same way.

During and after the Korean War (1950-53), the number of Catholic relief organization and missionary increased. The Korean Catholic Church grew

A Korean Catholic church celebrating mass

quickly and its hierarchy was established in 1962. The Roman Catholic Church in Korea celebrated its bicentennial with a visit to Seoul by Pope John Paul II and the canonization of 93 Korean and 10 French missionary martyrs in 1984. It was the first time that a canonization ceremony was held outside the Vatican. This gave Korea the fourth-largest number of Catholic saints in the world, although quantitative growth has been slow for Catholicism.

Protestantism

In 1884, Horace N. Allen, an American medical doctor and Presbyterian missionary, arrived in Korea. Horace G. Underwood of the same denomination and Methodist Episcopal missionary, Henry G. Appenzeller, came from the United States the next year. They were followed by representatives of other Protestant denominations. The missionaries contributed to Korean society by rendering medical service and education as a means of disseminating their credo. Korean Protestants like Dr. Seo Jae-pil, Yi

Dedicating a renovated Christian church

Sang-jae and Yun Chi-ho, all independence leaders, committed themselves to political causes.

The Protestant private schools, such as Yonhi and Ewha schools functioned to enhance nationalist thought among the public. The Seoul Young Men's Christian Association (YMCA) was founded in 1903 along with other such Christian organizations. The organizations carried out socio-political programs actively, encouraging the inauguration of similar groupings of young Koreans. These groups pursued not only political and educational causes but also awakened social consciousness against superstitious practices and bad habits, while promoting the equality of men and women, elimination of the concubine system, and simplification of ceremonial observances.

The ever-growing vitality of the Protestant Churches in Korea saw the inauguration of large-scale Bible study conferences in 1905. Four years later, "A Million Souls for Christ" campaign was kicked off to encourage massive new conversions to the Protestant faith. Protestantism was warmly received not only as a religious credo but also for its political, social, educational and cultural aspects.

Cheondogyo

Cheondogyo was initiated as a social and technological movement against rampant competition and foreign encroachment in the 1860s. At that time, it was called *Donghak* (Eastern learning) in contrast to "Western learning."

The principle of *Cheondogyo* is *Innaecheon* which means that man is identical with "Haneullim," the God of *Cheondogyo*, but man is not the same as God. Every man, bears "Haneullim," the God of *Cheondogyo* in his mind and this serves as the source of his dignity, while spiritual training makes him one with the divine.

Islam

The first Koreans to be introduced to Islam were those who moved to northeastern China in the early 20th century under Japan's colonial policy.

A handful of converts returned home after World War II, but they had no place to worship until Turkish troops came with the United Nations forces during the Korean War (1950-53) and allowed them to join their services.

Korean Islam's inaugural service was held in September 1955, followed by the election of the first Korean Imam (chaplain). The Korean Islamic Society was expanded and reorganized as the Korean Muslim Federation in 1967, and a central mosque was dedicated in Seoul in 1976.

Sports and Leisure

Traditionally, Korean people have enjoyed a variety of sporting activities and games. The impressive economic advancement of recent years has brought about a flourishing of interest in sports. More and more Koreans are now exercising and competing in organized sports.

In 1982, the Ministry of Sports was established to promote physical education and sports throughout the country and provide the necessary government assistance. The Sports Ministry was later integrated with the Ministry of Culture and Tourism.

The most noteworthy accomplishments in recent years include the successful hosting of the 1988 Seoul Olympic Games and co-hosting of the 2002 FIFA World Cup with Japan.

Considering the size and population of Korea, its performance in international sports competitions has been outstanding. Unprecedented in Asia, Korea has qualified for the World Cup finals six times.

The government implemented a Five-Year National Sports Promotion Plan (1993-1997) and invested 410 billion won to build 49 stadiums, 74 gymnasiums, 17 swimming pools and 1,728 neighborhood sports facilities. The government also developed cultural and sports centers in 21 farming and fishing towns.

With the completion of the First Five-Year Plan, a second phase was implemented from 1998 through 2002, with a budget estimated at three trillion won.

Korean skaters win gold medals at the 2002 Olympic Winter Games, Salt Lake, USA, February 2002.

The major objectives of the plan include the promotion of a "sports-for-all" movement nationwide, the advancement of elite sports, and the development of new sports technology and information to further foster sports industries.

To support various projects, the Korea Sport Science Institute is compiling a computerized database covering sports facilities, programs, coaching staffs and the public's participation rate in sporting activities.

One important aspect of the government's sports policies involves promoting interchanges with North Korea. The Korean government has long pursued participation in sporting events with North Korea, believing that sport is one of the most effective means of reconciling a divided people. In addition, the Republic of Korea supported bids for North Korea to join various international sports organizations such as the World Mountain Climbers' Association and the Pan-Asian Boxing Association.

The Seoul Olympics in Retrospect

The 24th Summer Olympic Games were successfully concluded after a 16-day run in Seoul, from September 17 to October 2, 1988, under the theme: Peace, Harmony, Progress. In what was the largest-ever Olympiad up to that time, more than 13,000 athletes and officials from 160 countries gathered to promote the lofty ideals of harmony and peace, while transcending the barriers separating East and West, and North and South. The first boycott-free Olympics in 12 years, the Seoul Olympic Games rose above ideological division and national interest, placing the Olympic movement back on the right track. The success of the Seoul Olympic Games was the result of the all-out effort the Korean people put forth to achieve harmony and peace for the entire human race, the undaunted spirit of the International Olympic Committee to revive the Olympics as a genuine festival for all mankind, and the aspiration for peace shared by nations around the globe.

Partly as a result of the 1988 Seoul Olympics, Korea now has many world-class sports facilities, concentrated in Seoul and Busan where most of the Olympic events were held. The Seoul Sports Complex, which encompasses a land area of 545,000 square meters, includes the Olympic Stadium with a seating capacity of 100,000, two gymnasiums for basketball and boxing, an indoor swimming pool, a baseball stadium and a warm-up field.

Olympic Park, occupying a vast area of some 1.5 million square meters in southeastern Seoul, comprises a 6,000-seat capacity velodrome, three gymnasiums, fencing and weightlifting venues, indoor swimming pools, and tennis courts.

A key training facility for the country's athletes is

Praising Olympic Flame in the 1988 Seoul Olympics

the Taeneung Athletes' Village, located on the eastern outskirts of Seoul. Built on a 17.1 acre site in the midst of a beautifully wooded area, the village includes a skating rink, indoor swimming pool, shooting range and gymnasiums for wrestling, boxing and weightlifting.

International Sports Competition

Korea is an active participant in many international sports competitions. Korea participated in the London Olympics in 1948 for the first time under its own national flag. In 1936, a Korean marathoner, Sohn Kee-jeong, won a gold medal in the Berlin Olympics, but he competed as a member of the Japanese team because Korea was under Japanese colonial rule at the time.

Korea's athletes have continued to improve their performances in Olympic Games. In the 1976 Montreal Games, Korea ranked 19th among more than 100 participating nations. In Los Angeles in 1984, Koreans captured 10th place out of 140 nations, and achieved fourth out of 160 nations in the 1988 Seoul Olympic Games.

Korea placed seventh in the final medal standings in the 1992 Barcelona Olympics. It was a memorable event for Koreans especially with Hwang Young-jo's gold medal in the marathon, enabling him to become the nation's first marathoner to win this Olympic event under the Korean national flag.

In the 1992 Barcelona Olympics, Korea placed seventh out of 172 countries with twelve golds, five silvers and twelve bronzes. Korea ranked 10th in the 1996 Atlanta Olympics with seven gold, 15 silver and five bronze medals, and 12th in the Sydney Olympics four years later with eight golds, nine silvers and eleven bronzes.

2002 FIFA World Cup Korea/Japan

The 2002 FIFA World Cup Korea/Japan ended its one-month epic event on June 30, 2002. The first FIFA World Cup of the 21st century consisted of a total of 64 matches and was safely completed without any hooliganism or terrorism that was feared might occur.

The national teams of Korea and Japan both cleared the first round of competition, and acquitted themselves valorously, the Japan team advancing to the final 16, and Korean team advancing through to the semi-finals. These successes were ones that until this tournament had never been achieved by an Asian country in the World Cup.

South Korean national soccer squad captain kicks the ball during a match in the 2002 FIFA World Cup.

The first ever co-hosted event in FIFA history, the 17th World Cup saw an outsider South Korea catapult into the semifinals for the first time to the astonishment of the world. The amazing performance of the Korean team improved Korea's national image dramatically, etching the brand "Korea" among people around the world.

The soccer event provided a good opportunity to shed Korea's negative images, associated with war, demonstrations and authoritarianism, as well as allowing the country to join the ranks of advanced countries.

The performance of the indefatigable Korean players was more than enough to impress the global audience and the outpouring of "Red Devils" across the country to support their team during the World Cup illustrated potent cohesiveness of the Korean people as a whole.

Since there were multiple sources of Korea's dynamic performance on and off the soccer field,

The Korean cheering squad, Red Devils

Korea may be on the threshold of a new economic takeoff. It certainly was high time for the government as well as the private sector to make the best of this hard-earned momentum.

Heaping praise on the Korean side for its amazing performance, foreign media said Korea was the biggest winner of the first world soccer championship in this century. The Korean people have also impressed foreigners with their enthusiastic and orderly "street cheering," which analysts say should be a model for the rest of the world.

A combined total of nearly 22 million people were estimated to had taken to the streets nationwide to cheer for the Korean national soccer team during its seven World Cup matches.

The numbers swelled to 4.2 million people for the final-16 match against Italy, 5 million for the quarter-final against Spain and 6.5 million for the semifinal against Germany. For the third-place match against Turkey on June 29, 2.17 million people showed up in the streets.

A total of 10.48 million people gathered in the streets of Seoul during the seven games, which accounts for 88 percent of the capital's population.

Since 1971, the Republic of Korea has annually sponsored an international football tournament, originally known as the President's Cup Football. The tournament, which has since been renamed the Korea Cup, has greatly contributed to the improvement of soccer skills in Asia and has promoted understanding and friendship among the participants. The tournament has drawn teams from Asia, Europe, Latin America and Africa. In 1983, Korea became the first country in Asia to field a professional football league. In 1994, the professional league changed its name to the K-League. Today, 10 teams compete in this league, which allowed foreign players' participation beginning in the 1996 season.

National Sports Events

The National Sports Festival is held every October featuring competition in 39 different sports by participants from all over the nation. The festival is held on a rotational basis in major cities, including Seoul, Busan, Daegu, Gwangju and Incheon.

The Children's National Sports Festival is also held annually for primary and middle school students, drawing over 10,000 boys and girls from across the country. The National Winter Sports Festival, held every January, includes speed skating, figure skating, skiing, ice hockey and biathlon.

Another annual event is the National Sports Festival for the Handicapped. Held each year since 1981, it brings people together from all over the country and provides the opportunity for these individuals to demonstrate their sports skills.

Korean-born Park Chan-ho pitching at a U.S. Major League baseball game; Pak Se-ri, winning the champion's trophy in an LPGA event

Skiing has fast become a popular winter sport among Korea's youth in recent years. Ski season in Korea is rather short, from late December to early March, during which shuttle buses run between outlying resorts and Seoul. Every February, the Foreigners' Ski Festival is held at the Yongpyeong Ski Resort, while several thousands of tourists from Southeast Asian countries visit Seoul in the wintertime to enjoy skiing and skating at resorts scattered throughout the country.

Others

Koreans also competed well among the top athletes in the Olympics as well as in other major international events, such as baseball, golf, archery, shooting, table tennis, short-track speed skating and ski jump.

Recently, Korean baseball stars have begun to make a name for themselves in American and Japanese leagues. After a rough start in the Major Leagues, Park Chan-ho is now a starting pitcher for the Texas Rangers and Kim Byung-hyun is piling up strikeouts with the Arizona Diamondbacks. Choi Hee-sup is active as an up-and-coming first-baseman for the Chicago Cubs, a U.S. Major League Baseball team.

In golf, Korea has recently produced many world-class players. In particular, professional female golfers such as Pak Seri, Kim Mi-hyun and Grace Park distinguished themselves by winning several LPGA or Women's US Open titles. Choi Kyung-ju charged his way to win two PGA titles in 2002 alone.

In tennis, Lee Hyung-taik became the first Korean man ever to win a major international event when he won the Addidas International tournament held in Sydney, Australia in January 2003.

Traditional Sports

Ancient Koreans were recorded to have engaged in numerous traditional sports games, such as kite flying, tug-of-war, *geune, jegichagi, neolttwigi* as well as *taekwondo* and ssireum. Kite flying is one of the most popular winter season sports when strong winds are prevalent. Traditionally, New Year's Day was set aside for flying kites of various shapes and colors.

Korean *tug-of-war* involves a large group of villagers participating in the contest, divided into two teams. Team members at both ends of a long thick rope, which was made of rice straw, pull on the rope, believing that the winning side would enjoy a good harvest that year.

Geune was popular among women, and is still being done mainly on *Dano* in May or June of each year. There are various styles of competition, including single-swinging and duo-swinging on two strands of rope suspended from high above.

Jegichagi, a game for boys, was normally played during the winter season. A shuttlecock was made of old coins with a hole in the center, which were

Taekwondo, a Korean art of self-defense, draws worldwide fans.

wrapped with paper or cloth, through which feathers were inserted and fanned out into a circle. The shuttlecock is kicked with one foot or both feet into the air, and the person who kicks it the most number of times without it touching the ground wins the game.

Neolttwigi resembles the Western game of seesaw. It involves a long board called *neol*, a full bag of rice or rice and straw mixture, is placed under the center of the board. Two girls in colorful traditional costumes stand on each end of the plank and bounce each other into the air alternately.

Among all other traditional sports that have been revived in modern times, the martial art of *Taekwondo* is the best known internationally and the only officially acknowledged international sport to originate in Korea, which is practiced worldwide.

Taekwondo uses the entire body, particularly the hands and feet. It not only strengthens one's physical well-being, but also cultivates character via physical and mental training, coupled with techniques for discipline. This self-defense martial art has become a popular international sport in the last quarter century, with some 3,000 Korean instructors now teaching *Taekwondo* in more than 150 countries.

Evidence of *Taekwondo*'s existence as a systematic defense method using the body's instinctive reflexes can be traced back to ceremonial games that were performed during religious events in the era of the ancient tribal states.

During religious ceremonies such as *Yeonggo, Dongmaeng* (a sort of Thanksgiving ceremony), or *Mucheon* (Dance to Heaven), ancient Koreans performed a unique exercise for physical training and this exercise led to the development of *Taekwondo*.

In Korea, the *Taekwondo* Association has a membership of about 3.8 million, constituting the largest affiliate of the Korea Sports Council. The World *Taekwondo* Federation (WTF), with its headquarters in Seoul, was officially approved as the governing body of the sport by the International Olympic Committee in 1980. *Taekwondo* was a demonstration sport in the 1988 Seoul Olympics, reflecting its worldwide popularity.

It became an official Olympic medal event beginning in the 2000 Sydney Olympics.

Ssireum, a Korean traditional form of wrestling, is a type of folk competition in which two players, holding on to a *satba* (a cloth-sash tied around the waist and thigh), use their strength and various techniques to wrestle each other to the ground. The history of *ssireum* began at the same time that communities began to form. In primitive societies, people inevitably had to fight against wild beasts, not only for self-defense, but also for securing food. In addition, it was impossible for these communities to avoid getting into conflicts with other tribes. As a result, people ended up practicing different forms of

Ssireum, Korean traditional wrestling, is a popular sports event.

martial arts to protect themselves.

The ultimate winner of a *ssireum* tournament was customarily awarded a bull, which was not only a symbol of strength, but also a valuable asset in an agricultural society.

In Korea today, *ssireum* has emerged as a sport with a large following, rather than a mere traditional folk competition conducted only on holidays. The Korean *Ssireum* Association has succeeded in generating a nationwide boom in this traditional sport by sponsoring highly competitive matches. Its popularity, as one of the favorite spectator sports in the nation, is such that matches are regularly broadcast on TV so that people can enjoy matches from their homes. With the development of consistent rules and guidelines, *ssireum* has continued to progress from a traditional sport and self-defense method into a well-loved folk competition and popular modern sport that is a part of the lives of Koreans today.

Leisure

The leisure industry is one of the fastest-growing

Koreans enjoying professional baseball and basketball.

sectors in Korea, as an increasing number of people engage in various leisure activities as a result of the nation's rising living standards. Koreans, by nature, are outgoing and engage in leisure activities with as much intensity as they do work. The many museums, palaces, temples, royal tombs, parks and scenic and historic sites found all across Korea have always been popular sites for family outings and picnics. In recent years, many people seem to find physical exercise as a good way of spending their free time while promoting their overall well-being.

Tennis and jogging are the two most popular morning sports. Those who are more athletically-oriented organize morning soccer teams. Among other activities pursued are swimming, hiking, golfing, skiing, water skiing, salt- and fresh-water fishing, wind surfing and handball. Spectator sports like soccer, baseball, basketball, volleyball, boxing and *ssireum* all have avid followings.

Recently, more and more urban residents have tended to spend their holidays away from home.

Mountain climbing in the winter

With the rapid increase in privately-owned automobiles, more families travel out of the city to the mountains and beaches on weekends and during holidays. At the same time, watching television and playing *janggi* (Korean chess) or *baduk* (go game) remain popular ways of spending weekends among many male office workers.

Especially on almost every weekend, mountains and hills in the suburbs of cities are filled with hikers and mountaineers. Since Korea's Ko Sang-don climbed the summit of Mt. Everest in September 1977, the number of mountaineers and hikers has markedly increased in recent years. Considering the fact that about 70 percent of the Korean territory is covered with mountains, and the Korean people's love of nature, this nationwide enthusiasm for climbing stands to reason.

Tourism

With its scenic beauty and unique cultural and historical heritage, Korea has much to offer international tourists. A peninsular country with four distinct seasons, the nation boasts picturesque valleys, mountains, rivers and beaches. Throughout the country there are numerous ancient temples and shrines, royal palaces, sculptures, pagodas, archeological sites, fortresses, folk villages and museums. Recently, travel between South and North Korea was launched, and other sightseeing programs under co-sponsorship with the North Korean authorities are also anticipated in the near future.

Moreover, due to its high-quality facilities and favorable geographic conditions and climate, Korea has recently gained a great deal of popularity as a site for winter sports, especially in East Asia. Korea hosted the Asia-Europe Meeting (ASEM) in October 2000, the General Assembly of the World Tourism Organization (WTO) in September 2001. The World Cup soccer, one of the most exciting sporting events in the world, took place in 10 major cities each in Korea and Japan from May 31 to June 30 in 2002. Moreover, Korea is making great strides towards its goal of becoming a prime tourist destinations.

Korea's tourism industry has been growing by leaps and bounds over the last three decades. The number of foreign visitors increased from 173,335 in 1970 to 5.1 million in 2001. The development of Korea's tourism industry is a natural consequence of

View of Seoul City

its phenomenal economic growth, but the specific allocation of resources has also been a vital factor. The government enacted a series of tourism promotion laws which resulted in an average growth rate of 5.0 percent annually in tourist arrivals over the last decade.

There have been massive projects to develop tourism resources and facilities such as accommodations, transportation, tourist services, national parks, museums, golf courses and casinos. Increasing numbers of tourist guides, proficient in English, Japanese, Chinese and other languages, are being trained and deployed. Most of the tourism development and promotion projects have been spearheaded by the Korea National Tourism Organization (KNTO).

The composition of the nationality of tourists arriving in Korea has been shifting over the last three decades, from Americans to Asians. In 1970, Americans accounted for 32 percent of inbound tourists, while Japanese formed the second largest group. By 2001, however, visitors from Japan accounted for 46.2 percent of the total, followed by visitors from China at 9.4 percent, making them the second largest group. Visitors from the United States comprised 8.3 percent of the total.

Getting to Korea

Arrival by Air:

Korea is connected by air to every major capital in the world, either through direct flights or by connecting flights from major international airports in East Asia. About 37 international airlines maintain regular flight services, with over 1,500 flights into and out of Korea every week. Korea has four international airports: Incheon International Airport in Incheon, which began its operation on March 29, 2001, plus Gimhae, Jeju-do and Cheongju International Airports in Busan, Jeju Island and in Cheongju. Gimhae and Jeju operate direct flights to and from Tokyo, Fukuoka, Nagoya and Osaka in Japan.

Korean Air (KAL), the largest of Korea's two national flag carriers, has opened new routes between Seoul and destinations in Europe, America and the Middle East. The Korea City Air Terminal (KCAT), located next to the Korea World Trade Center in Samseong-dong, provides check-in service, passport clearance and airport departure tax tickets. Nonstop limousine buses make round trips between Incheon International Airport and KCAT every 10 to 20 minutes. Another KCAT opened recently at Gimpo International Airport.

Special airport buses and city buses leave from various points in Seoul every 15 minutes from 5:00 a.m. to 10:30 p.m., as less expensive alternatives to the KAL Limousine Bus line which connects Incheon International Airport with 19 major hotels in Seoul.

Incheon International Airport

Since 1963, Seoul has been included in the round-the-world air schedule approved by the International Air Transport Association (IATA). This enables any passenger on a round-the-world ticket to visit Korea at no additional charge.

Arrival by Ferry:

Various steamship lines provide passenger service to Korea. Among those from the American West Coast are Waterman Steamship, American Pioneer, Pacific Far East, Pacific Orient Express, State Marine and United States Lines. Several companies, such as the BuGwan Ferry, Korea Ferry and Korea Marine Express, provide regular ferry services linking Busan and Jeju-do Island with the Japanese ports of Shimonoseki, Kobe and Hokada. Another ferry line plies between Incheon and the Chinese ports of Tianjin and Weihai.

Temporary entry for private cars is allowed for passengers arriving by ferry, providing that drivers obtain the proper documentation.

View of Mt. Bukhansan

Exploring Korea

Seoul

Located along the Hangang River, Seoul, the capital city of Korea, has grown into a teeming metropolis with a population of more than 11 million. While maintaining and restructuring the city, which has greatly expanded in the process of urbanization and industrialization, it continues to grow as the prosperous and thriving center of the country's political, economic, cultural and educational activities.

Seoul is the world's 10th-largest city; its past and present coexist in a fascinating way. Centuries-old palaces, gates, shrines, gardens and priceless art collections in museums attest to the illustrious past of the city, while the glistening facades of soaring skyscrapers and the bustling traffic represent its vibrant present.

Old Seoul was encircled by four inner mountains and four outer mountains. The four inner mountains,

Mt. Bugaksan in the north, Mt. Naksan in the east, Mt. Inwangsan in the west, and Mt. Namsan in the south, refer to those which were originally inside the castle walls of the ancient capital of the Joseon Dynasty (1392-1910). The four outer mountains are Mt. Bukhansan in the north, Mt. Yongmasan in the east, Mt. Deogyangsan in the west, and Mt. Gwanaksan in the south. Each mountain has a unique beauty of its own while boasting natural scenic landscapes and spectacular views overlooking the city of Seoul. There are also numerous mountain springs that are clean to drink from and resting spots for people hiking along these mountain areas.

In Seoul, the must see attractions are the four ancient royal palaces dating back to the Joseon Dynasty: *Gyeongbokgung, Deoksugung, Changdeokgung*, and *Changgyeonggung. Jongmyo* Shrine, the royal ancestral shrine of Joseon, along with *Huwon* (the Rear Garden), adjacent to *Changdeokgung*, are noted for their beautifully landscaped gardens and classical structures. One of the most popular areas for foreigners is Insa-dong, located near

Insa-dong in the most visited place by foreigners

Citizens enjoying pastime at the theme park Lotte World in Seoul.

downtown Seoul, which is lined with antique shops, art galleries, traditional teahouses, and restaurants as well as bookstores. It is a place that beckons both casual shoppers and the serious collectors.

Other attractions highly recommended for foreign visitors include the National Museum, the National Center for Korean Traditional Performing Arts, the Sejong Center for the Performing Arts, the Ho-Am Art Hall and Korea House. The National Museum of Contemporary Art in Gwacheon, a southern satellite town, also deserves a visit.

From Mt. Namsan Park, in the heart of Seoul, visitors can enjoy a panoramic view of the entire city from Seoul Tower, or view a recreation of traditional village.

There are an abundance of parks within and around Seoul, such as Olympic Park, Seoul Grand Park and Citizens' Forest, providing not only places to relax, but also a variety of walking, riding and cycling opportunities. These parks are among the hidden treasures of Seoul, enjoyed by residents but often missed by tourists.

Another experience visitors should definitely not pass up is a Korean dinner, either at a modern restaurant or a courtly Korean-style restaurant. Excellent Chinese and Japanese food is also available, as well as French, Italian, Mexican, Pakistani and many other cuisines.

Seoul also has an active nightlife with bars, cafes, and rooftop nightclubs. The fantastic night scenery of Seoul can be experienced through a river cruise along the Hangang River which meanders through the heart of the city.

Seoul Vicinity

Gyeonggi-do Province is located in the western central region of the Korean Peninsula, with the Hangang River running through its center. The river divides the province into a mountainous northern area and open fields of its southern area. While Seoul keeps its visitors busy with so many intriguing and enticing things to see and do, this area outside of Seoul can provide a refreshing and invigorating break.

Suwon Fortress, registered on UNESCO's World Cultural Heritage list

Korean Folk Village in Yongin

The shoreline of coastal regions juts in and out along the beaches and includes countless gulfs, peninsulas and islands. Namyangman Gulf, Asanman Gulf, Gimpo Peninsula, Hwaseong Peninsula, Ganghwado Island, and Yeongjongdo Island are all attractions that visitors cannot afford to miss. Symbolizing prosperity, the golden bell, the provincial flower of the province, flourishes widely throughout the area.

Within a 30-minute drive to the south of Seoul is Korean Folk Village. This traditional village reenacts the everyday Korean life of days gone by. It opened in 1973 and now includes aspects of almost everything traditionally Korean. Homes typical of the various provinces are on display. In the village square tightrope walkers, wedding and funeral processions, kite-flying contests and folk dance troupes are presented regularly. The blacksmith, carpenter, potter and craftsman can be seen at work in their shops. Adjacent is Hwaseong Fortress, a walled city of the Joseon Dynasty which was recently included on

UNESCO's prestigious World Heritage List.

Yongin Everland, a comprehensive leisure complex, comprises state-of-the-art amusement facilities, including water parks and spa facilities, for ideal summer recreation for all age groups.

The distinguished Ho-Am Art Museum displays over 5,000 pieces of art. About 80 kilns are concentrated in the area of the Icheon Ceramic Festival which is held in September each year, where you can savor the mysterious color of Goryeo celadon and the white purity of Korean porcelain.

Ganghwado Island is situated in the estuary of the Hangang River north of Incheon Port. This is Korea's fifth-largest island, an area rich in history and natural beauty. Major historic monuments here include an altar said to have been erected by Dangun, the legendary founder of Korea, along with fortresses, ancient walls, a celadon kiln dating to the 13th century Goryeo period, and *Jeondeungsa* Temple.

Just a 56 km bus trip north of Seoul is Panmunjeom, the truce village where the Korean Armistice Agreement was signed on July 27, 1953, ending the fierce fighting of the Korean War (1950-53). It is

Icheon Ceramic Festival takes place every September.

now a joint security area managed by the U.N. Command and North Korean guards. Visitors, escorted and briefed by military guides, can easily sense the tension pervading all the facilities and persons on duty.

Eastern Region

Gangwon-do Province is located in the central eastern area of the Korean Peninsula. Most of the land is covered with thick forests providing an abundance of scenic vistas with fewer residential areas than in other provinces. Both its remote wooded mountains and ravines and small coastal towns are rich in scenic splendor.

With these natural conditions, Gangwon-do was the ideal site for the 4th Asian Winter Games in January 1999. The International Travel Exposition '99 was also held from September 11 through October 30, 1999. Over 2 million visitors from overseas as well as all around the country participated in these events. Under the theme, "Man, Nature and Life of the Future," it hosted not only fascinating exhibitions but provided useful information and presented a wide array of performances and events for visitors throughout the Expo period.

The eastern coastline, stretching 390 kilometers (234 miles) from Hwajinpo to Busan, is rugged and mountainous with breathtaking scenery. Skiing and other winter sports help make the area a year-round resort destination. To meet the needs of more than one million skiers per year, several ski resorts are now equipped with snow-making machines, which have extended the ski season from December to March. Other popular recreational activities in the region include swimming in summer and mountain climbing in autumn. The beaches here are perhaps

Seoraksan National Park in Gangwon-do Province

the finest in Korea, gently sloping into shallow water and mild currents.

Mt. Seoraksan, which is part of the Mt. Geumgangsan Range, draws visitors with its magnificent splendor.

It is also inhabited by the half-moon bear, Gangwon-do's symbolic animal and one of the most endangered species in the world. Mt. Seoraksan, is truly an impressive and colorful all-season destination.

Other tourist sites include Cheoksan Hot Springs and Unification Observatory, which is located along the south bank of the estuary of the Hangang River and Imjingang River and offers an excellent view of the North Korean territory abutting the DMZ along the stream.

Chuncheon, the capital of Gangwon-do Province, holds the Chuncheon Puppet Festival in August every year, which features the active participation of puppet theater groups from around the world.

Mt. Geumgangsan, the magnificent "diamond mountains"

Ulleungdo Island, lying 268 kilometers (161 miles) northeast of Pohang, is an extinct volcano rising prominently from the East Sea. Dokdo Island, the most easterly point of Korea, lies 92 kilometers (55 miles) to the southeast.

Mt. Geumgangsan is one of the most scenic tourist spots on the Korean Peninsula and considered one of the world's most spectacular natural wonders. It is located in North Korea near the eastern end of the Demilitarized Zone, dividing the peninsula. Luxury cruise boats capable of carrying some 1,000 tourists travel from Donghae in the South to the North's eastern port of Jangjeon, where the tourists take chartered buses to the mountain.

Central Region

The province encompassing Chungcheongbuk-do and Chungcheongnam-do lies in the western center of the peninsula. Chungcheongbuk-do is the only landlocked province. With the completion of the government complex in Daejeon and the newly opened

Gosudonggul Cave

inter-national airport in Cheongju, the provincial capital of Chungcheongbuk-do has grown rapidly into not only a strategic heartland of the domestic economy but also an international gateway for the mid-region of Korea.

Daejeon is situated about two hours by car south of Seoul, a major train junction for the Seoul-Busan and Seoul-Gwangju-Mokpo lines. It is rapidly developing into one of Korea's major scientific centers. Expo Park, the site where the Daejeon Expo '93 was held, has been renovated and converted into a public science park.

Buyeo, the final capital of the Baekje Kingdom (18 B.C.-A.D. 660), features the comprehensive collection of the Buyeo National Museum which houses about 7,000 relics from the Baekje period.

Mt. Gyeryongsan, one of the nation's five most famous mountain sub-ranges, is located in the province with the Geumgang River flowing alongside. As the original center of Baekje culture, the area abounds with unique cultural artifacts and historic relics.

In addition to the natural scenic sites provided by numerous peaks and saddlebacks along the ridgeline of the Sobaeksan Mountains, there is a wealth of National Treasures and historical places as well.

These include the Seven-Story Stone pagoda, iron flagpole of Yongdusa Temple, Palsangjeon wooden Pagoda, Sangdangsanseong Fortress, Hyeonchungsa and Yi Chungmugong Chungnyeolsa Shrine. Moreover, many other celebrated temples, statues, national parks and hot springs are waiting to be discovered.

Chungjuho Lake offers a variety of delightful water sports in the mountainous area of central Korea. Cruise boats ply between Chungju and Danyang allowing passengers to enjoy stunning views of *Danyang-Palgyeong*, the "Eight Scenic Wonders." Gosudonggul cave captivates visitors with its glistening stalactites in all shapes and sizes. Chungju orchards are one of the main sources of excellent quality apples in Korea. Yellow tobacco is also a specialty of this region, while its ginseng has gained a worldwide reputation.

Southwestern Region

Korea's southwestern region encompasses Jeollabuk-do and Jeollanam-do, which was originally the main part of the Baekje Kingdom. The region is relatively flat, containing broad stretches of rice paddies, and its jagged coastline creates many small harbors. It is a fertile and warm region sheltered by high mountains on the east and north and calm seas and many islands on the west and south. Because of the influence of both continental and ocean climates, the province exhibits a wide variety of weather conditions.

Jeonju is famous for its traditional mixed vegetable rice dish *bibimbap*, and for *hanji*, traditional mulberry paper. The provincial bird is the magpie, which is related to a poignant legend. According to this legend, on the night of the seventh day of the seventh

Paik Nam-june's Art in the Gwangju Biennale

lunar month, magpies build a bridge above the Milky Way by carrying twigs and pebbles in their beaks, allowing two lovers who are destined to meet only once a year, *Gyeonu* and *Jingnyeo*, to see each other again.

Namwon is the gateway to Jirisan National Park, as well as the famed home of Chunhyang, one of Korea's most celebrated national heroines. *Chunhyangga*, a Korean traditional narrative epic *pansori* about the faithfulness of her love, is one of the most favored performances in Korea. Jirisan has the second highest mountain peak in the Republic of Korea. The sub-range is vast in size and stretches across three provinces, Jeollanam-do, Jeollabuk-do and Gyeongsangnam-do.

Deogyusan National Park commands superb views of the 30 kilometer-long *Mujugucheondong* Valley. The valley encompasses Muju Ski Resort, the largest skiing area in Korea. The Gwangju National Museum is home to a collection of Chinese ceramics recovered from a 600-year-old Chinese merchant ship that was wrecked in the seas off Sinan.

Damyang, 22 kilometers north of Gwangju, is the center of bamboo cultivation and craftsmanship. Damyang Bamboo Museum is the world's first museum devoted exclusively to bamboo.

Other cultural attractions, historic sites, and museums such as Hwangtohyeon Victory Field, Gochang-eupseong Fortress and Gangam Calligraphy Museum also give the province much of its rich character.

On Jindo Island, which is some 350 kilometers south of Seoul, visitors can see the Korean version of Moses' Miracle. The sea between the coastal village of Hoedong-ri on Jindo Island and nearby Modo Islet actually does part for about an hour twice a year in early May, and again in the middle of July, leaving a walkable path, 2.8 kilometers long and 40 meters wide. Jindo Island is also renowned for its Jindotgae, an indigenous Korean breed of dogs, designated Natural Monument No. 53.

Southeastern Region

Korea's southeastern region, encompassing Gyeongsangbuk-do and Gyeongsangnam-do, is an

Wondrous separation of water near Jindo Island

Gyeongju, known as an open-air museum, is full of cultural artifacts.

area rich in tourist attractions with a great diversity of cultural assets and historical places. Hallyeosudo Waterway, and the Jirisan and Gayasan mountains are outstanding natural tourism resources in this region.

Gyeongju, which was the ancient capital of the thousand-year Silla Kingdom (57 B.C.-A.D. 935), is now an exceptional open-air museum. Royal tombs, temple sites with weathered stone pagodas and Buddhist reliefs and fortress ruins are scattered all around the city. The mounded royal tombs have yielded many precious antique objects including exquisite gold crowns and other accessories.

The two supreme treasures of Gyeongju are the Bulguksa Temple and nearby *Seokguram* Grotto shrine, both completed in the eighth century and representative of highly refined Buddhist art widely appreciated throughout East Asia. They were included on UNESCO's World Heritage List in 1995. Other important historic sites include: *Dumuli Park, Oreung* (Five Tombs), *Cheomseongdae* (observato-

Hahoe village still maintains a traditional lifestyle.

ry), General Kim Yu-sin's Tomb, and Mt. Namsan, which is dotted with numerous Buddhist images, pagodas and temple remains. The Gyeongju National Museum houses antique treasures recovered from Gyeongju and its vicinity.

Bomun Lake Resort, located 6 kilometers from downtown on the eastern outskirts of the city, is an integrated tourist destination with several first-class hotels and various recreational facilities. Haeinsa Temple is famous for housing the 80,000 wooden printing blocks used to print the *Tripitaka Koreana*, which were carved in the 13th century. The *Tripitaka Koreana* is acknowledged as the most complete compilation of Buddhist scripture in East Asia.

Not far from historic Gyeongju are the growing industrial cities of Pohang and Ulsan. Pohang is home to the POSCO steel mills, while Ulsan is the industrial base for Hyundai, one of Korea's leading conglomerates. Busan is Korea's principal port and second-largest city. The Jagalchi Fish Market is right next to the piers where fishing boats unload their hauls daily. A colorful spectacle in the early morning, it is a great attraction for tourists as buyers haggle over the catch of the day.

Andong is one of the last living vestiges of old Korea, a treasure-trove of Confucian tradition. Hahoe, a small village near Andong, is famous for its unique traditional masks and the mask dance-drama, *Hahoe-talchum. Dosanseowon*, a Confucian academy founded by one of the most well-known scholars, Yi Hwang, in the 16th century, is also nearby. Massive-scale international tour and resort complexes are due to be completed by 2006 in the western and northern areas, featuring ultramodern recreation and leisure facilities. Hundreds of thousands of visitors are expected to flock to the area to visit them.

Jejudo Island and Southern Coastal Regions

Within an hour's flight from Seoul, Busan or Daegu, travelers in Korea can reach a land of a completely different character, recognized as the best preserved and most unspoiled area in the nation, Jejudo Island, Korea's only island province.

The island is Korea's most popular tourist resort as well as its most favored honeymoon destination. Known as "Little Hawaii" for its volcanic landscape, picturesque subtropical scenery, sandy beaches, waterfalls and hiking trails, it is one of the world's top 10 tourist attractions with over 4 million visitors a year.

Jejudo enjoys a semitropical climate, with its plants and landscape being remarkably different from those of the mainland. It is also the natural habitat of over 2,000 species. Its principal mountain is the 1,950-meter-high Mt. Hallasan, an extinct volcano with a large crater. Lava flows from this volcano, last active in 1007, have resulted in many tunnels, pillars and other unusual features formed of the quick-cooled

Coastlines on Jejudo Island, known for their serene beauty.

basalt. Tourist sites include the Jeju Folkcraft and Natural History Museum, Jungmun Resort, Cheonjiyeon Falls and Jeju Fantasy Gardens, with several representative gardens from around the world.

Jejudo Island offers visitors a great chance to glimpse the island's unique folk culture, especially through its thatched-roof houses. They reflect both the island's natural environment, characterized by strong winds, and the lifestyle of the island people, renowned for their generosity and warmth.

Most of the rivers in Korea have their tributaries in the northern and eastern regions and flow west and south. Concentrated for the most part along the southern coast are more than 3,000 islands providing grand scenery with a convoluted coastline. The completion of the Honam and Namhae expressways in 1973 made these picturesque coastal routes more easily accessible.

The areas around Jinhae, Tongyeong, Jinju and Namhae are recommended as highlights of this scenic region. The southern boundary of the Korean

Snow-covered Mt. Hallasan on Jejudo Island

Peninsula is a sunken coastline which has created an irregular pattern of bays and inlets with more than 400 offshore islands. Beyond the expressway and rail service, a cruise on the hydrofoil between Busan and Yeosu is recommended; it stops at Seongpo, Tongyeong, Samcheonpo, and Namhae.

Travel Advice

General Information: Tourist information and assistance are available at all major tourist sites and airports including KNTO's (Korea National Tourism Organization) Tourist Information Centers. They are open everyday from 9 a.m. to 6 p.m. (November to February from 9 a.m. to 5 p.m.) KNTO is also running a tourist information site on the web (www.tour2korea.com) Since around a quarter of the Republic of Korea's resident population may be on the move to visit hometown and family during traditional national holidays, it is advisable to make travel and accommodation arrangements at least three months in advance for those periods. The busiest holidays are Lunar New Year's Day, summer vacation (the last week of July through the third week of August), and *Chuseok* (The 15th day of the Eighth Month by the lunar calendar).

During national holidays offices and banks are closed, whereas palaces, museums, most restaurants, markets, department stores, cinemas and amusement facilities are usually open.

A variety of local events, festivals and special performances such as *sandaenori* (mask dance) and *nongak* (farmers' music) are held in many locations all year-round, welcoming foreign visitors.

Reservations for hotels in any part of the country can be made in Seoul through travel agencies. Foreign tourists can get an instant assistance by dialing 1330 anywhere in Korea.

Guided Tour Services: Guided tours around Seoul's scenic attractions and historic sites are offered regularly by various travel agents. A wide variety of tours are available, including morning, afternoon and night tours as well as nationwide tours of a week or more in duration.

Currency: Korea's currency unit is *won* which comes in 1,000, 5,000 and 10,000 *won* bills, and 10, 50, 100 and 500 *won* coins. Generally, banks are open between 09:30-16:30 Monday to Friday. Automated teller machines are in operation 24 hours a day. Most larger stores, hotels and restaurants in Korea will accept major international credit cards. However, it is advisable to carry some cash, since many smaller establishments and stores are unlikely to accept any credit cards.

Visas: Tourists may visit Korea for 15 days without a visa, but proof of confirmed onward air reservation is required. Nationals of certain countries do not need visas and may remain up to three months in some cases, 1 or 2 months in others, provided they do not engage in remunerative activities while in Korea. In the case of a special long-term visa, visitors are required to apply for alien registration at a local immigration office within 90 days of arrival.

Animal and Plant Quarantine: All imported animals, plants and their products are subject to quarantine at airports and ports of arrival at the time of entry.

Accommodations

Visitors to Korea can choose from a wide range of good-value accommodations including hotels, inns, hostels, homestays and resort condominiums. There is an extensive choice of hotels: super deluxe, deluxe, first, second, and third class. Rates start at about 46,000 *won* per night, and in the case of deluxe hotels, room charges go up from about 170,000 *won*.

An increasing number of hotels offer recreation facilities such as swimming pools, saunas, indoor driving ranges, bowling alleys and health clubs for their guests. There are also disco and karaoke bars, casinos and recreation rooms, providing nighttime as well as daytime entertainment. In addition, exciting and fun-filled special seasonal events and packages are available throughout the year.

Inns and hostels are inexpensive types of accommodations. They offer simple, clean accommodations. Rates vary with the services and facilities provided. Staying at hostels can cost as little as 6,000~22,000 *won* per night and inns range from 30,000 *won* to 60,000 *won*.

Homestays offers not only relatively cheap or sometimes even free lodging but a great opportunity to make friends with a Korean family and personally experience the Korean lifestyle as well.

Resort condominiums provide excellent self-service accommodations and are mostly located in cities with major tourist attractions. They are fully equipped with kitchens, bedrooms, bathrooms and so on, and available also to non-members on a short-term basis.

How to Travel Around Korea

Domestic flights: Korean Air and Asiana Airlines provide domestic air transport service, connecting Seoul with other major cities, involving one-hour flights at most. They also connect Jejudo Island with major cities in Korea.

Gimpo Airport is used for domestic flights only, while Incheon International Airport had replaced it as the gateway for international flights.

Railway services: The Korean National Railroad operates super-express, express and local trains along an extensive network covering almost every corner of the country. Super express trains link Seoul with Busan, Mokpo, Gyeongju, Gwangju and Yeosu. Most popular destinations in the nation can be reached with mostly single-change connections. The super-express and express trains include dining cars connected to overnight trains. Local trains make frequent stops.

Bus services: Intercity bus networks connect virtually all cities and towns in the country and are an economical way to travel. Exclusive bus lanes are enforced in the daytime, which makes it less time-consuming to travel by bus. Local, city and express buses with fares between 500 to 1,400 *won* service all cities small or large. City buses are numbered according to their routes, but since signs are usually in Korean and no English timetables are available, it is advisable to know the bus numbers in advance.

Long distance express buses: Two services, regular express buses and deluxe express buses, provide efficient access to all major towns in Korea. Deluxe buses offer spacious seats and amenities such as mobile phones and VCRs. Late-night deluxe express buses run on some lines. The Seoul Express Bus Terminal and the East Seoul Express Bus Terminal are the two busiest terminals in Seoul, and are both located in the central part of city. Busan's Express Bus Terminal is located in the eastern part of downtown.

Subway services: The subway is the most efficient and convenient way to get around Seoul, Busan and Daegu. The subway system has developed into these cities' main transport system and continues to provide a fast, safe, and comfortable means of transportation. In Seoul, it links all neighborhoods with the outlying areas and satellite cities. On the intercity network, trains operate at intervals of 2.5 to 3 minutes during the morning and evening rush hours, and intervals of 4 to 6 minutes during non-peak times. Fares vary according to destinations, with a basic fare of 700 *won*.

Taxi services: There are two kinds of taxis - regular and deluxe. Fares are based on distance and time. The fare for deluxe taxis is somewhat higher than that of regular taxi, but nearly all taxis are equipped with a third-party interpretation system that can be accessed by cellular phone.

Car rental: Driving in Korea can be an exciting and effective way of getting around. An extensive road and expressway network is available, which means you can visit every corner of the country.

Road numbers and destinations are clearly indicated on road signs. Drivers must meet the following requirements: one year of driving experience, an international driver's license valid for a year from the date of entry, at least 21 years of age, and valid passport.

Rental fees vary from 68,000 to 265,000 won for a day, depending upon the type of car. The speed limit is 60km/hr for most roads in the city and 80-100km/hr for city expressways including Olympic Expressway. Driving while intoxicated involves a very heavy penalty.

Ferry Services: This offers one of the most pleasant ways to see Korea. Routes are available between Busan and Jejudo Island, Mokpo and Hongdo Island, and Pohang and Ulleungdo Island. A hydrofoil runs between Busan and Yeosu on the south coast, calling at several small ports along the way.

Shopping

The Republic of Korea is known as a Mecca for shoppers, offering a great variety of items at reasonable prices. Tourists may purchase many necessities and souvenir items of both domestic and foreign origin tax-free at any of the hundreds of shops in department stores and shopping arcades in Seoul as well as major cities throughout the country.

Popular shopping items include jewelry, furs, silk, antique chests, ceramics, lacquerware, brassware, embroidery, personal computers, video and cassette tapes, sportswear, down winter coats, eel skin and leather products, ginseng and dolls. Major department stores located in the heart of Seoul and include Shinsegae, Lotte, Midopa, Samsung Plaza and Hyundai. Also branch department stores can be

Myeong-dong shopping district in downtown Seoul

found in many other areas, often located nearby a subway station.

A network of underground arcades branch out from Myeong-dong, Seoul's most popular shopping and entertainment area. Many subway entrances and underpasses also lead to a maze of tunnels with shops aimed at bargain hunters. Of all commercial areas in Seoul, however, Itaewon, which is located adjacent to the major U.S. military compound, bustles with the greatest number of overseas visitors. Insa-dong, or Mary's Alley, is clustered with many fabulous antique and art stores.

With thousands of shops and stalls, divided section by section according to category of item, *Namdae mun* and *Dongdaemun* Markets are the largest general wholesale markets in Korea. They are renowned for offering an inexpensive, wide variety of everyday items. Tourists will easily find any number of things to buy in these markets, which will accommodate all tastes and budgets. Between midnight and 4 a.m., retail merchants from all over the country come to restock their stores, presenting the bustling spectacle of a nighttime wholesale market.

There is also a wide variety of specialty markets in Seoul, including Gyeongdong Market, a health

Gyeongdong market attracts visitors with its Oriental medicine and health supplements.

supplement and Oriental medicine specialty market, and the largest electronics market in Asia, Yongsan Electronics Market. Although most large open-air markets in Korea are closed on Sundays, other large-scale discount stores and department stores are always open all weekend.

For more information

- Korea Travel Phone: area code+1330
- Seoul Information Center: (02)731-6337
- Korea National Tourism Organization: (02)757-0086
  http://www.knto.or.kr
- Call taxis: (02)414-0150/5
- Seoul Express Bus Terminal: (02)535-4151
- Railroad Information Center: (02)735-5678
- Incheon International Airport: (032)741-0104
- Korea City Air Terminal: (02)551-0077
- Korean Air: (02)656-2000
- Asiana Airlines: (02)669-4000
- Tourist Complaint Center: (02)735-0101

http://www.korea.net

Visit **korea.net**, the official website of the Korean
Government, whenever you need:

- An update of what's happening in Korea.
- In-depth knowledge about Korea's
  Economy, History, Arts and Culture.
- The latest Government Information.
- An extensive directory of websites related to Korea.

Korea.net provides users with the most accurate,
timely, and comprehensive information about Korea.

20 Korean Cultural Features

Hanbok: Traditional Korean Dress

The women's hanbok comprises a wrap-around "chima" skirt and bolero-like "Jeogori" jacket. The men's consists of a short "Jeogori" jacket and "baji" pants.

Both ensembles may be topped with a long coat of a similar cut called "durumagi." Today, people wear hanbok mostly on festive days or for ceremonies like a wedding or funeral.

Kimchi and Bulgogi: Health Food

Bulgogi, which literally means fire meat, is popular dish among Koreans, while kimchi, a fermented vegetable dish, provides a spicy contrast. Bulgogi can be made of any kind of meat, although beef and pork are the most popular.

Seasoning is important for the right taste of bulgogi as it is for kimchi. Kimchi can be made with various kinds of vegetables, with the most common being cabbage and radish kimchi. The vegetables are pickled in salt water and rinsed. After the water has dried a bit, the cabbage and radish are seasoned. Kimchi is low in calories and cholesterol and very high in fiber. It is richer in vitamins than apples. One might thus say "some kimchi a day keeps the doctor away."

Hangeul: The Korean Alphabet

Created in the 15th century by Joseon King Sejong, Hangeul consists of 14 consonants and 10 vowels. The combination of a consonant and a vowel forms a syllable and thus,

Hangeul is capable of creating thousands of words and expressing virtually any sound. Because of its simplicity and relatively limited number of characters, Hangeul is easy to learn. Illiteracy is almost non-existent in Korea thanks to the ease of learning this alphabet.

Jongmyo Jeryeak: The Music of Jongmyo Ancestral Rites

On the first Sunday in May of each year, descendants of the Jeonju Yi clan, the royal family of Joseon (1392-1910), honor their ancestors in elaborate rites at the dynasty's Jongmyo Shrine in downtown Seoul.

Although the ceremony is conducted in a much-abbreviated form, as many as 19 different classical musical instruments, including stone chimes, bronze bells, and various drums, are played to produce very special music for the traditional ceremony.

Masks and Mask Dance-Dramas

Masks, called "tal" in Korean, were made of paper, wood, gourd and fur. They mostly reflect the expressions and bone structures of Korean faces but some represent deities and animals, real and imagined. Their shapes were grotesque and greatly exaggerated, because "talchum," the mask dance-drama, was usually performed at night in the light from wood fires.

Mask dance-dramas are basically a folk art which naturally developed among the common people of Joseon who shared a sense of alienation from the ruling elite and upper social classes.

In most cases, the actors and spectators joined together in robust dance at the end of a performance.

Korean Ginseng

Ginseng is widely cultivated in Korea where the climate and soil produce the world's finest quality. To distinguish it from ginseng grown in other parts of the world, Korean ginseng is called "Goryeo ginseng" after the ancient dynasty of Goryeo, from which the English name "Korea" was derived.

Ginseng is used as a restorative or tonic. It has been traditionally believed that ginseng strengthens vital organs, stimulates the heart, protects the stomach, enhances stamina and calms nerves. Ginseng is a core ingredient in Oriental medicine but Koreans take ginseng in an easier way in the form of tea or liquor.

Bulguksa Temple and Seokguram Grotto

Bulguksa, one of the largest and most beautiful Buddhist temples in Korea, is located in Gyeongju, once the capital of the ancient Silla Kingdom (57 B.C.-A.D. 935). Bulguksa originated as a small temple that King Beop-heung (r. 514-540), the first Silla monarch to embrace Buddhism, had erected to pray for the prosperity and peace of his kingdom.

The temple's present structures date back to 751 when they were rebuilt. The temple previously comprised more than 80 buildings, 10 times the number surviving today. Situated high up on the mountain behind Bulguksa is Seokguram, a man-made stone grotto widely regarded as one of the world's finest Buddhist grottos.

Seokguram comprises a rectangular antechamber and a round interior chamber with a domed ceiling connected by a rectangular passageway. Seokguram and Bulguksa were registered on the UNESCO World Cultural Heritage List in 1995.

Mt. Seoraksan

Korea has two beautiful mountains-Seoraksan in the South and Geumgangsan in the North. Seoraksan is the southernmost extension of the legendary Geumgangsan or Diamond Mountains in the North.

The forests of Seoraksan, whose highest peak rises to 1,708 meters above sea level, are a luxurious mix of deciduous broad-leaved trees with alpine plants and conifers, which are home to about 939 different species of plants, 25 species of mammals, 90 birds, 11 reptiles, 9 amphibians, 360 insects, and 40 freshwater fish.

Korean Artists

Koreans exhibited their excellence in the field of music and the arts.

Violinist Sarah Chang recorded her first album when she was nine.

Another outstanding Korean violinist, Chung Kyung-wha has been and remains one of the most sought-after musicians on the international stage for more than 25 years.

Soprano Jo Su-mi was discovered by the world-famous conductor Herbert von Karajan who praised her as having a "God-given voice."

It may be a surprise to many that Paik Nam-june, the Korean-born "father of video art," began his career as a musician and composer.

In 1963, he became the first person to exhibit "prepared" television sets. Since then, Paik has influenced contemporary art, video and television with works linking the worlds of art, media, technology, pop culture and the avant garde.

Printing Heritage

Woodblock printing began in the 8th century in Korea. The world's first metal typeface was developed by Koreans more than 200 years before Gutenberg of Germany.

People of the Goryeo Dynasty (918-1392) produced *Tripitaka Koreana* in the 13th century, recognized as the world's oldest extant woodblocks of Buddhist scripture. The *Tripitaka Koreana* has been listed on the World Cultural Heritage List of UNESCO since 1995.

Traditional Musical Instruments

There are approximately 60 traditional Korean musical instruments that have been handed down through the generations. They include the 12-string zither "gayageum" and the six-string zither "geomungo," both presumed to have originated before the sixth century.

Traditional Korean instruments can be broadly divided into three groups-string, wind and percussion. The Kim Duk-soo Samullori percussion quartet is quite well-known in and outside Korea for its dynamic combination of traditional rhythms and modern compositions which create a unique musical experience.

Dancheong : Decorative Patterns on Buildings

Dancheong refers to Korean-style decorative colored patterns used on buildings and other items to convey beauty and dignity.

For dancheong, five colors are used: red, blue, yellow, black and white. In addition to its decorative function, dancheong was applied for practical reasons as well.

It was used to protect building surfaces and conceal any crudeness in the quality of the material used, while emphasizing the characteristics and representing the grade or rank that a building or object commanded. Dancheong can be found on most traditional buildings, including temples, whether they are in Seoul or provincial areas.

Patterns

Patterns often have their origins in early ideographs. They began as a means to express basic needs and feelings about one's surroundings and developed into a universal form of decorative art.

Among the most common patterns used in traditional Korea are the dragon and phoenix, and "taegeuk," used in the Korean national flag Taegeukgi, consisting of two contrasting elements of eum and yang which symbolize such cosmic forces as tranquility and activity, weakness and strength, darkness and light, and male and female.

Also common are the ten longevity symbols: rocks, mountains, water, clouds, pine trees, turtles, deer, cranes, fungus of immortality and sun.

Jasu : Embroidery

Embroidery was widely applied on clothing and ornamental items such as folding screens. It was also used to decorate numerous items used in the home, including pillow cases, eyeglass containers, cushions and pouches for such things as tobacco, spoons and chopsticks, and brushes.

Common people were not allowed to wear embroidered clothing, except for ceremonial dress worn for weddings. Unlike embroidery for purely decorative purposes, Buddhist jasu, which decorated temples and statues, was created out of religious devotion.

Paper Crafts

Koreans have a time-honored tradition of paper-making and have long enjoyed using indigenous high-quality paper for making wardrobes and trunks, bowls with lids, large bowls, baskets, mesh bags, jars and trays.

Other popular items include stationery cases, mats, cushions, curtains, quivers, dippers, powder-flasks, footwear, washbasins and chamber pots. Most of these paper products were carefully varnished to enhance their appearance and durability while making them waterproof. The most commonly used varnish was a mixture of unripened persimmon juice, rice glue and perilla oil.

Bojagi : Wrapping Cloths

Bojagi refers to square hemmed cloths of various size, color, and design, which Koreans used to wrap, store, or carry things.

Bojagi are still used nowadays, though less frequently. Although they were created for daily use, bojagi added flair and style to ceremonies and rituals.

Korean artistic flair is reflected especially in patchwork bojagi made by housewives so as not to waste small, leftover pieces of cloth. Embroidery figures and characters make bojagi even more charming. When it is not in use, bojagi can be folded into the size of a small handkerchief.

Folk Paintings

Folk paintings comprise works which were widely used by commoners in ancient Korea to decorate their home or to express their wishes for a long happy life.

Unlike the noble class paintings that usually focus on landscapes, flowers and birds, folk paintings abound with humor and simple and naive ideas about life and the world.

Folk paintings were produced by artists who obviously belonged to a low social class, but their paintings were used by people of all social strata, from the royal household and temples down to farmers in remote villages. The paintings are characterized by their bold composition, dynamic brushwork and intense colors.

Sesi : Seasonal Customs

Sesi customs include ceremonial rites that are observed on days of seasonal turning points, prescribed in the lunar calendar. For instance, on New Year's Day, Koreans enshrine their ancestral tablet and hold a memorial service with food and wine offerings. After the service, there is "sebae" or deep, formal bows to senior members of the family. On the eve of the 15th day of the First Full Moon, called "daeboreum," a straw effigy was made and then thrown into a stream. This practice has ceased in many parts of the country, but the tradition of preparing and eating a variety of seasonal vegetable dishes is still widespread. The 15th day of the eighth month is Chuseok, a sort of Thanksgiving Day, when people visit their ancestral gravesites for memorial services. One of the special dishes prepared for this day is "songpyeon," the half-moon-shaped rice cakes that contain sesame seed, beans, chestnuts or other fresh crops.

Rites of Passage

In Korea, the stages that an individual goes through in life and the accompanying changes are collectively known as "Gwanhonsangje," covering coming-of-age, marriage, funeral and ancestor worship. The coming-of-age rite was simple. Boys have their long hair tied into a topknot and are bestowed a *gat*, a traditional Korean hat made of horsehair. Girls have their hair braided into a chignon and fixed with a long ornamental hairpin called binyeo. Marriage ceremonies were performed at the bride's home and the newlyweds usually spent two or three days with the bride's family before going to the groom's home.

Funeral rites were played out in complex formalities in traditional Korea. Mourning usually lasted for two years, following a strict protocol involving a series of prayer rites observed during the period. In addition to elaborate funeral rites, Koreans have inherited a rich tradition of ancestral worship services that provide a connection between the dead and the living.

Gardens

The essential concept behind the Korean art of gardens is to make the garden setting look more natural than nature itself. In many cases, what appears to be the work of nature turns out, upon closer look, to be the result of very conscious efforts.

The best preserved among all ancient palace gardens is Anapji pond in Gyeongju, Gyeongsangbuk-do. Also of unparalleled beauty is the garden of Changdeokgung Palace in Seoul, comprising some 300,000 square meters of the entire 405,636 square meters of the palace grounds. The garden is tastefully laid out with picturesque pavilions and halls, lotus ponds, rocks, stone bridges, stairways, water troughs and springs scattered among dense woods, all essential elements of a traditional Korean garden.

The Executive Branch

Office of the President
http://www. president.go.kr

Office of the Prime Minister
http://www.opm.go.kr

Board of Audit and Inspection
http://www.bai.go.kr

National Intelligence Service
http://www.nis.go.kr

Ministry of Gender Equality
http://moge.go.kr

Presidential Advisory Council for Science and Technology
http://www.pacst.go.kr

Fair Trade Commission
http://www.ftc.go.kr

Financial Supervisory Commission
http://www.fsc.go.kr

Ombudsman of Korea
http://www.ombudsman.go.kr

Commission on Youth Protection
http://www.youth.go.kr

Ministry of Planning and Budget
http://www.mpb.go.kr

Ministry of Legislation
http://www.moleg.go.kr

Government Information Agency
http://www.allim.go.kr

Korean Overseas Information Service
http://www.korea.net

Patriots and Veterans Administration Agency
http://www.bohun.go.kr

Ministry of Finance and Economy
http://www.mofe.go.kr

National Tax Service
http://www.nts.go.kr

Korea Customs Service
http://www.customs.go.kr

Public Procurement Service
http://www.pps.go.kr

National Statistical Office
http://www.nso.go.kr

Ministry of Unification
http://www.unikorea.go.kr

Ministry of Foreign Affairs and Trade
http://www.mofat.go.kr

Ministry of Justice
http://www.moj.go.kr

Supreme Public Prosecutors' Office
http://www.sppo.go.kr

Ministry of National Defense
http://www.mnd.go.kr

Military Manpower Administration
http://www.mma.go.kr

Ministry of Government Administration and Home Affairs
http://www.mogaha.go.kr

National Police Agency
http://www.npa.go.kr

Ministry of Education and Human Resources Development
http://www.moe.go.kr

Ministry of Science and Technology
http://www.most.go.kr

Meteorological Administration
http://www.kma.go.kr

Ministry of Culture and Tourism
http://www.mct.go.kr

Ministry of Agriculture and Forestry
http://www.maf.go.kr

Rural Development Administration
http://www.rda.go.kr

Forestry Service
http://www.foa.go.kr

Ministry of Commerce Industry and Energy
http://www.mocie.go.kr

Small and Medium Business Administration
http://www.smba.go.kr

Intellectual Property Office
http://www.kipo.go.kr

Ministry of Information and Communication
http://www.mic.go.kr

Ministry of Health and Welfare
http://www.mohw.go.kr

Food and Drug Administration
http://www.kfda.go.kr

Ministry of Environment
http://www.me.go.kr

Ministry of Labor
http://www.molab.go.kr

Ministry of Construction and Transportation
http://www.moct.go.kr

National Railroad Administration
http://www.korail.go.kr

Ministry of Maritime Affairs and Fisheries
http://www.momaf.go.kr

National Maritime Police Agency
http://www.nmpa.go.kr

The Legislature

National Assembly of the Republic of Korea
http://www.assembly.go.kr

Local Governments

Seoul Metropolitan Government
http://www.metro.seoul.kr

Busan Metropolitan Government
http://www.metro.busan.kr

Daegu Metropolitan Government
http://www.daegu.go.kr

Incheon Metropolitan Government
http://www.inpia.net

Gwangju Metropolitan Government
http://www.metro.gwangju.go.kr

Daejeon Metropolitan Government
http://www.metro.daejeon.kr

Ulsan Metropolitan Government
http://www.ulsan.go.kr

Gyeonggi-do Province
http://www.kg21.net

Gangwon-do Province
http://www.provin.gangwon.kr

Chungcheongbuk-do Province
http://www.cb21.net

Chungcheongnam-do Province
http://www.chungnam.net

Jeollabuk-do Province
http://www.provin.jeonbuk.kr

Jeollanam-do Province
http://www.jeonnam.go.kr

Gyeongsangbuk-do Province
http://www.gyeongbuk.go.kr

Gyeongsangnam-do Province
http://www.provin.gyeongnam.kr

Jeju-do Province
http://www.jeju.go.kr